ACKNOWLEDGEMENTS

It is my pleasure to express gratitude
to the following professionals for their input and
assistance regarding this book:

Jack Ryan, Dr. Virginia Mayer, Joanne Petras,
Joe Carter, Lisa Mays, Edouard Sooh, Shermane Willis,
Jimi Ballard, Denise Pringle and Russell Hall.

DEDICATION

To Ginger

A LAND OF MYSTERY, MAGIC AND MAYHEM:

Reflections on Japan by One Who Lived There During the MacArthur Occupation

J.D. Taylor

Copyright © 2013 John D. Taylor
All rights reserved. No part of this publication may be reproduced, stored in or introduced into a retrieval system, or transmitted in any form, or by any means (electronic, mechanical, photocopying, recording, or otherwise), without the prior written permission of both the copyright owner and the publisher of this book. For information address Hudson House Publishing.

ISBN 13: 978-1-58776-946-7

Library of Congress catalog card number: 2013954352

Manufactured in the United States of America

675 Dutchess Turnpike, Poughkeepsie, NY 12603
www.hudsonhousepub.com   (800) 724-1100

Contents

	Historical Forward	i
	Introduction	1
I	A Bridge to the Past "...Man is a Bridge and Not a God"- Nietzsche, *Thus Spake Zarathustra*	5
II	Background and Travel to the Land of the Rising Sun "To Love Oneself is the Beginning of a Life-long Romance" – Oscar Wilde	11
III	Truth "The Smallest Atom of Truth Represents Some Man's Bitter Toil and Agony" – H. L. Mencken	19
IV	The Element of Surprise "All the Business of War...is to Find Out What You Do Know" – The Duke of Wellington	45
V	Loyalty "Animals Are Such Agreeable Friends – They Ask No Questions, They Pass No Criticisms"– *Mr. Gilfil's Love Story*	61
VI	MacArthur to Ridgeway "Duty is Like a Man's Shadow; it Follows Wherever You Go" – Marcus Aurelius	65
VII	Life at Camp Sendai: Mr. Tucker's History Class "Education Makes People Easy to Lead, But Difficult to Drive, Easy to Govern, But Impossible to Enslave" – Baron Brougham, 1778-1868	77
VIII	Sayonara "Goodbye, Tired World! I'm Going Home. Thou Art Not My Friend and I'm Not Thine." – Ralph Waldo Emerson	115

Historical Forward

Postwar Japan was physically benumbed, rudderless, ill-clothed and hungry. Japan had two trajectories into the future: democracy or totalitarianism which is a canker on the body politic. Japan was set for Armageddon prior to the Emperor's unconditional surrender speech.

General Douglas MacArthur, motivated by his sense of duty, was supremely confident holding his shield of faith and sword of truth as he inspired the Japanese people during a most difficult time, giving them hope and direction for a better future. He carried out the most radical of reforms without raising an eyebrow, an adumbration of the future.

Japan advanced in the arena of democracy, women's rights and a free press. MacArthur, in a word, fashioned a "Second Opening." Japan was once again open to systemic change.

MacArthur asserted by dint of hard work, ravaged cities like Tokyo needed to be rebuilt. He also insisted on land reform thus eliminating a system where a favored few were able to batten in extreme comfort while others toiled. Likewise, a secular state was established, police departments decentralized and reorganized. Labor unions were created, railroad service revived and the arms industry dismantled. Then, the antiquated Shinto-based educational system requiring only six years of schooling was updated to

K-12 and new Vocational, Technical and University level schools were inaugurated.

Above all, MacArthur's reforms set forth the notion of government by law—and not by men. The Tokyo War Crime Trials (1948) hanged seven war criminals and purged thousands of high military and civilian officials, a condign punishment for all. And life expectancy over time rose for men to 69 years and for women to 74 years.

The one downside to MacArthur's reforms, however, was the polarization of political parties causing factions, the same factions described by James Madison in *Federalist Papers #10*. Factions became diverse political parties which in turn created what Karl Marx called the "class struggle" that led to the unequal distribution of private property—an inevitable consequence of capitalism.

MacArthur's occupied Japan was somewhat different from occupied Germany. Japan was not directly governed by foreign troops as was Germany. Instead, Japanese "prefectures" contained The General's military teams which ensured that the reforms were carried out by the rule of law, an example of indirect democracy. At MacArthur's GHQ in Tokyo were various staff sections parallel to the ministries in the Japanese governmental structure.

The 1947 Constitution was prefaced in part on the Meiji Constitution which renounced the horrors of war and Japanese militarism.

MacArthur understood that a democratic Japan would become a strategic geopolitical ally and serve as a bulkhead against the wave of isolationism and Soviet totalitarianism.

General Douglas MacArthur rebuilt Japan in his own image with a competitive capitalist economy and a free-speaking society for the first time ever.

Introduction

In some way, writing is a Sisyphean task in that one never knows when a work is whole or complete. An epiphany enlightened me when I began searching bygone years realizing the essence of my existence, in a distant magic land of so long ago called Japan.

My story is told in three perspectives: a child maturing in MacArthur's Japan, an adult narrating first-hand life experiences deeply swayed by those amazing years and as a historian bringing to light the significance of this stretch of time.

In addition, the narration delves into essential historical occurrences concerning China, Korea and America that played decisive roles in shaping Japan's social, political, economic and culture, past and present.

Most of all, I endeavor to explain how Japan's impact upon those countrys' history changed my daguerreotype of MacArthur's Japan. It was Louie Daguerre (1789-1851) who made a major contribution to American history by his invention of the daguerreotype (1839), the earliest version of photography which has served to preserve the visual history of America.

Today, I set my eyes on the fact that my idealistic childhood Shangri-La was locked in a conundrum: an incomprehensible contrast between the beauty of an advanced culture versus the mayhem and evil of World War II atrocities and subsequent reckless slaughter of whales, dolphins, sharks and Blue Fin tuna.

Japan, once a country of vast irrigated rice paddies, produced enough rice to sustain its dense population. Not today, unfortunately. Extra rice has to be imported. Rice agriculture commands the development of patterns of cooperative labor which transfers sociologically towards a regimented social order. The individual is forced into a group structure that makes regimentation a *fait accompli* with resulting alienation from other societies, which in turn leads to isolation, an unfortunate component of Japanese history.

In feudal Japan, Confucianism put emphasis on the political-social order. Confucianism meant discipline, ethical self-cultivation and high political consciousness necessary for stabilizing the country. Confucianism's influence, however, began to fade after Commodore Perry's collision with the 200-year-old isolationist barrier (1853-54).

As a result, Japan eventually became "cultural-borrowers" of Western innovations—even baseball! The belief that Buddhism possessed mystical powers provided a vehicle which transferred much Chinese culture to Japan. Buddhism's appeal was based upon its reputation as a magical protection of families and of the state. Families, therefore, built protective family temples.

By the ninth century, Buddhism had spread to all parts of Japan. In addition, Buddhism introduced new concepts of afterlife, charity, service and a prejudice against the eating of meat.

One of the many mysteries regarding Japan lies in the fact there are Buddhist injunctions against the taking of life, be it human or animal. Why, then, the warlike ferocity of "bushi" or "Samurai" (the warrior code) that drove the Japanese to commit gratuitous violence against humanity during World War II? Does the answer lie in the notion that militarism became absorbed into and dominated the political and economic systems?

Fifty percent of the American people today feel that our best days are behind us; this startling reality inspired me to look into my past and good fortune to have lived in MacArthur's Japan (1949-52).

General Douglas MacArthur was ideal to become the Supreme Commander for the Allied Powers (SCAP) in charge of the entire occupation. He viewed himself as a man of destiny, a lead actor on the stage of history.

MacArthur, although a Catholic, was an Existentialist. He insisted on freedom of choice and being responsible for one's actions. And for me, a young lad of twelve years, MacArthur was my hero. His Japan elevated my spirits in both a spiritual and Existentialist way, much like Buddhism did for the Japanese.

Buddhism introduced me to a method of meditation, discipline of character, a form of individualism independent of authority and a sense of salvation through self-understanding .

Because I rever MacArthur, old Japan and this era of history, my cultural and philosophical mindset began to evolve for my life's journey as a compassionate, educated and responsible adult with deep emotions, serious thoughts and a propensity towards meaningful actions.

My angst of the power of death was assuaged while reflecting upon John Donne's "Death, be not proud," when he said: "And Death shall be no more; Death, thou shalt die."

The bell, says Donne "…doth toll for him that thinks it doth.…"

JD Taylor   *A Land of Mystery, Magic and Mayhem*

A Bridge to the Past
"...Man is a Bridge and Not a God"- Nietzsche, *Thus Spake Zarathustra*

I

By some touchstones, sixty-one years is an eternity. By others, it's a mere blip on the time continuum. A half-century or more often diminishes one's mind—or, it can unlock a treasure trove of memories buried deep in the sands of time. The latter is the case of my memory as I reflect upon the yearbook of my early life, a series of snapshots about life in MacArthur's occupied Japan 1949-52. Memories are a lifeline to the past and must be kept alive.

Jolting my remembrance are the gut-wrenching photos of the devastating earthquake and tsunami in 2011 that submerged Sendai, Japan, where I had lived for nearly two years. It is somewhat comforting to know that my former city of Sendai is receiving immediate help from her sister city of Riverside, California. It was President Eisenhower in 1957 who announced this program as a way to promote international cooperation at the local level. In fact, according to *The New York Times National* (March 20, 2011, 24) the United States has more sister cities in Japan than any other country, 188 in all.

These tragic events compelled me to tell my story, notwithstanding dark episodes in my earlier life, prior to my family's departure to the "Land of the Rising Sun" also known as "Land of Cute" and in Japanese, "Kawaii."

I could hear reverberations of John Paul Sartre's admonitions: "We are all responsible for the world; there are no excuses." Miyagi prefecture and Sendai will never be the same.

"The past and the future shed light on the present," said Existentialist philosopher Heidegger. My recollections are an emotional transport from the heart sustained by passion and spirit while searching for a catharsis. My passion for books, the arts, history, writing, suffering animals, environment and for life itself burst forth in MacArthur's Japan.

"Passion is what makes life meaningful," said philosopher Nietzsche. He also said passion is necessary for insight, clarity and creativity. Passion is the hope of life. Nothing great happens without passion.

Passion inflamed me as a young person, and led to my quest as to who I am and what I might become. Passion and spirit set the stage for my future, my self-identity and the possible meaning of my existence.

I was a Humane Investigator and teacher in the Commonwealth of Virginia for more than 30 years. I performed my court-appointed duties in my "spare" time and at my own expense, while I worked as a full-time history teacher at the local high school, an adult education institution and at a local college as an adjunct instructor. I considered my vocation as an avocation despite the long hours with both day and night school. The night school adult ed principal hired me to teach high school English, which I loved, especially my course in standard grammar and composition.

During this cycle, I became the focal point in two momentous occurrences: one involving a traveling zoo, the other, a hitchhiker dying with AIDS. There were many other occasions during my teaching career when I was able to rescue hundreds of suffering animals and become a partner in writing humane laws and speaking before members of the Virginia General Assembly on behalf of animal rights.

These seminal events defined my persona and became a psychological platform for my future as a responsible, empathetic and caring adult, qualities rooted in my formative years in MacArthur's Japan.

The Washington Post published a lengthy piece that I wrote explaining my actions in taking control of two tractor trailer loads of suffering, exotic traveling zoo animals. It is called "The Day the Wonder Zoo Came to Town: It Wasn't the Best Time to Walk an Ostrich."

Having legal power, I took a major risk in usurping the authority of Fairfax County Animal Control because Animal Control was about to allow these suffering animals to proceed to their next show in West Virginia. "Not on my watch!" I bellowed.

These creatures were owned by a profit-orientated vivarium from Florida, strictly out to squeeze the almighty dollar for as long as possible, despite animals suffering from malnourishment, heat exhaustion, hoof rot and worse.

Most notable was Nora, a baby elephant, 300-pounds underweight with an atrophied leg. There was also a cruelly treated 320-pound boa constrictor and an abused ostrich.

After many hours and the help of the county police, media, a district supervisor, and numerous outraged animal groups, we eventually re-located these creatures to the Reston Pet Farm in Reston, Virginia.

Finally, the U.S. Department of Agriculture (USDA) suspended the company's license and the Fairfax County Supervisors indicated that I acted lawfully. In addition, the Board passed a resolution that requires a permit prior to any future traveling zoos in the county. To date, I have not seen or heard of another traveling zoo.

Years later, another transformative experience gave impetus to my self-identity and existence by a heart-warming occurrence involving Toby Swenson and his beautiful dog named Hanna.

Toby and Hanna were hitchhiking their way from Lake Charles, LA, to their home in Pawtucket, R.I. Toby was dying from AIDS. Toby and Hanna were exhausted and weak when I discovered them in an underpass under the Capital Beltway on a red-hot August morning in Alexandria, VA. They were in need of immediate help. It was Toby's dream to arrive home in Rhode Island to attend his sister's wedding and eventually die there.

But he would not part with Hanna. Hitching with a dog was most difficult. He said Hanna had kept him alive for so long. I provided them with aid and comfort for three days. Later on, I received assistance from Mary Wadsworth, an employee with the Fairfax County Human Development Department, and Nancy Herndon who drove Toby and his dog to the vet and human hospital in preparation for their flight to Rhode Island. She later drove them to National Airport in Washington, D.C.

During his final days, Toby, wearing a tuxedo, with his beloved dog on a leash, attended his sister's wedding. Shortly thereafter Toby died in peace. Hanna was adopted by his best friend.

Arguably *The Metamorphosis* best identifies the importance of self-identity. Kafka deals with one who struggles with the unknown and with change, as I did in my first year in Japan. My little brother and I were stranded in a foreign land without parents. Our dying mother was one hundred miles south of Camp Jinmachi and our father on his way to Korea. It is still a Kafkaesque nightmare of mine, realizing in the present how I struggled with an illogical world without meaning and living by arbitrary rules I did not understand. Feelings of estrangement, loneliness, fear and alienation all bordered on futility and hopelessness.

Spiritual health and self-identity are defined by the relationship between body and soul which encouraged me to explore the core of my innerself. Without meaning and coherence, life was otherwise intolerable.

MacArthur's Japan and a subliminal exposure to Japanese Buddhism gave impetus to these dynamics. Buddhism taught me that ignorance and desire are factors that cause suffering, a concept that has plagued and intrigued me all through my life.

Those years stir a cauldron of emotions and a sense of having lived in a special historical interval, in a real-life Shangri-La, despite the barbarous acts of a people guided by the "Spirit of Bushido" – the spirit of the warrior, their belief in a god-like emperor and their zeal to ward off further Western domination in their struggle for modernization.

The "Spirit of Bushido" does not tolerate second chances – not at all. The first strike has to be successful or else it is considered a failure. That is why Pearl Harbor (1941) led to the Japanese attack on Midway Island (1942) as an attempt to salvage the "mistake" at Pearl Harbor of not sinking the four American aircraft carriers, the heart of the American navy which was out to sea. Japanese Admirals Nagumo and Yamamoto did not know this at the time.

The Japanese bombed Midway, then they went after the carriers. But the carriers were once again out to sea, undetected by Japanese scout planes. Midway was a major turning point in the war which eventually led to Japan's unconditional surrender (1945). Following the strict "Code of Bushido," Admiral Nagumo took his life for his dereliction.

Many Asians at this time saw Japan's war as their conflict as well: a clash of race, color, ideology and a sense of xenophobic nationalism or xenophobic delirium. Xenophobia is difficult for Japan to avoid as the Japanese are among the most racially homogenous people in the world. Japanese have often associated foreigners with crime, treachery and general unpleasantness. They were further alerted by a statement from Tyler Dennett (1922), an expert on Far Eastern affairs, who said: "Each nation, the United States not excepted, has made its contribution to the welter of evil...."

In Shakespeare's "King Lear," tragedy identifies principles of good that co-exist with evil. Perhaps political negotiations with Japan in 1941 could have ended with peace rather than war. As historian John Toland (*The Rising Sun*) says "...America would not have been forced to become the moral policeman of Asia...particularly when its own morality is in question."

America's disastrous war of aggression in Vietnam may have been avoided. Toland further points out that human nature and not history repeats itself. On his deathbed in Walter Reed Army Hospital, MacArthur beseeched President Lyndon Johnson not to get bogged down in Vietnam and to avoid Asian wars.

It is axiomatic that far too many American wars since 1945 (like Korea and Vietnam) have been presidentially driven, which is unconstitutional. James Madison wrote on Congress's role during times of war: "In no part of the Constitution is more wisdom to be found than in the clause that confides the question of war or peace to the legislature and not the executive...."

General Douglas MacArthur's Japan was the gold standard of postwar military occupation, despite facing many socio-economic and political issues, a tormented people and a human disaster created by the mushroom clouds of "Little Boy" and "Fat Man," creating the "fire of a thousand suns." But, as MacArthur was well aware, the Japanese are survivors. The Toyotas and Hondas attest to their ability to land on their feet. Recently, a 93-year-old man was discovered to have survived both A-bomb attacks. Tsutomu Yamaguchi has been certified "hibakusha" or radiation survivor of both Hiroshima and Nagasaki. Yamaguchi, a former Japanese businessman, was on a business trip when the first A-bomb was dropped. He suffered severe burns, spent the night in Hiroshima but went on to his hometown of Nagasaki just in time for the second blast. According to military records, Yamaguchi is one of some 260,000 Japanese who survived the bombings.

Viktor Frankl (a Holocaust survivor himself) said most people can withstand almost any suffering if they have a *raison d'etre* – a reason – to give their lives meaning and purpose.

MacArthur had plans for a new era, a constitutional era – with an emphasis on women's rights (even though The General was the epitome of a so-called male chauvinist and the idea of women's rights also quite foreign to this once Imperial power). MacArthur governed Japan through the Diet, the cabinet and the Emperor. He preserved the continuity of government. The Japanese were actually led by their own politicians and civil service.

By continuity, I mean MacArthur made the new constitution an addendum to the much older Meiji constitution. The General felt continuity was important to this occupied land. Essentially, the new constitution was really "The MacArthur Constitution." Much of this legislation was drafted on the sixth floor of the Dai Ichi Building, MacArthur's GHQ command center in Tokyo.

Background and Travel to the Land of the Rising Sun
"To Love Oneself is the Beginning of a Life-long Romance" – Oscar Wilde

II

Travel preparations for my Japanese journey began in 1948 including numerous immunizations covering every possible disease. I dreaded the shots. They really hurt. Most of them burned and created muscle soreness, nausea and vertigo. After receiving United States Army travel orders in May of 1949, my mother, brother and I began packing hold baggage which preceded our travel date.

Throughout my early life, I often left school before completing that particular grade. I attended twelve different schools in my K-12 academic career, including an incomplete tenure at a Catholic grade school in Colorado. According to psychology professor Shigehiro Oishi: "We know that children who move more frequently are more likely to perform poorly in school and have more behavioral problems." Professor Oishi goes on to say that long-term effects of moving from one place to another have significant deleterious consequences for adulthood. His research is based upon 7,108 adults, all subjected to being shifted about as children (many military brats like myself). The survey pointed to a resulting serious lack of social skills and relationship failures as adults. These subjects have a tendency for characterologic neuroses feelings of inferiority and introversion.

Professor Oishi and colleagues further concluded that far too many of us have been overlooked by societal institutions such as schools and classified us as misfits and malcontents, attributes that I have been accused of.

After reading this article published in the fall 2010 edition of *The University of Virgina Magazine* (one of my schools), I came away with a little more compassion for my enigmatic personality and the tangled emotions that have at times plagued my adult life.

I have a better understanding of my flaws such as introversion, feelings of inferiority to superiority, unsuccessful marriages and relationships (with both males and females) which eventually sent me to Anger Management School. Even then, I tried to take over the class as I felt the instructor had weak pedagogical skills. Animals, nature and books have always been my retreat and refuge as I zigzagged my way through time.

Professor Oishi's observations have given me an uplift and further insight into that gold mine of the past, helping me to continue my story and understand why I was a discontent as a young Catholic school student in Colorado Springs.

My resistance to regimental control did not set well with the nuns. They would often poke me with a ruler to sit straight or pay attention – even when I was paying attention with good posture. Granted, my mind often drifted when religious discussions permeated the classroom atmosphere. I was not that interested as I have always had an inner life of my own and never wanted to follow the "flock." I needed to free myself from the common ruck. That is why I never embraced any religion, even though I was baptized in the Catholic Church. Bells, candles and so-called holy water on my forehead seemed meaningless and superfluous.

My "free-spiritness" is affirmed by Nietzsche who said religious constraints should not hinder intellectual development. Like Nietzsche, Freud and Marx, I see organized religion as an opiate and a form of the "herd instinct" which thwarts individualism and stifles creativity and authenticity.

My Catholic school career ended shortly after my first failed confession. Father asked me about my sins. My retort: "You first, Father." Martin Luther would have been pleased because he believed that man did not need an intermediary (a priest) to communicate with God – nor did I. I was banished to public school with a blush of dishonor and sense of relief.

In May, my family departed for Ft. Lewis, Washington, home of the 2nd Infantry Division and our port of embarkation. The tarry at Ft. Lewis was brief but the days were occupied with lectures on how we

Americans should accept the Japanese as equals and not as conquered people. But there was one minor downside: While at Ft. Lewis I was told, much to my surprise, that because of post-war slim budgets, it was recommended that troops and even dependents like me and others awaiting embarkation to Japan, use only two, that is two sheets of toilet paper upon each visit to heed nature's call!

We would live on newly constructed military bases with adequate housing, and have access to the amenities of most Army camps such as a movie theater, gym, dispensary, hospital (not in all locations), and a Post Exchange (PX).

Assignments farther north of Tokyo and Yokahama, we were told, would have fewer accommodations. As such, I did not expect luxury living. But was I surprised! You bet! As previously stated, we had very comfortable quarters and a spacious yard, even though my stepfather was only a Sergeant First Class or E-6.

Some of the lecture sessions at Ft. Lewis included historical background on the coming of World War II and the Japanese involvement therein. Being young, the historical data captured my interest in a big way. I knew then that my curiosity would serve me well as I grew academically. Precocious, no. Interested, yes! Precocious children are average children of below-average parents.

A profound trauma of my journey happened at Ft. Lewis and has stayed with me well into adulthood. My mother and little brother were assigned a special, small private room with two beds. They were on the passport as "Taylor." I was listed as "Wojtacha," my Polish birth name. Evidently, my stepfather had adopted my younger brother but not me! Stunned, I was in mute disbelief. It was not a *Kumbaya* moment in my young life. As a result, I was sent to a dorm-like facility downstairs, away from my mother, partly because of my size, age and name. I did not like being separated and sleeping in a cavernous room with other boys, some of whom taunted me because of my curled blond hair and the way I was dressed. I was regarded by some as a "sissy." Actually, I felt like one. I also felt isolated, rejected and insecure, not only from the other young kids, but especially from my immediate family. That isolation has plagued me to this day. It reminds me of Paul Simon lyrics: "They've got a wall in China...to keep out foreigners...I've got a wall around me you can't even see...."

Shakespeare's empathy and insight into isolation is evident in one of his later plays, "Coriolanus." This Roman king suffered a tragic flaw like MacArthur: hubris. Tribunes eventually banished their king (as President Truman banished MacArthur) because he had become a dictator and had no compassion for the lower classes, the Plebeians. Upon his ejection, Coriolanus railed: "I am not a beast. Man does not live in isolation." The king's cry echoed my crushed emotions and despair.

My mother was of Italian descent (2nd generation) and dark as was my brother and stepfather. I was an antithesis in that I was very blond, blue-eyed, pudgy, anti-social and timorous. Not being adopted was catastrophic news to me. I was chagrined and crestfallen.

Daytime activities at Ft. Lewis were meaningful and complete. But nightfall presented a different climate for me. Feeling sullen and like a pariah, I withdrew and isolated myself even more. I did not go to the dorm. Instead, I slept the first night under a stairwell. Once my mother discovered my hiding spot, she smuggled me into her room the next night. The din of solitude was comforting.

My biological father and mother divorced when I was five years old. His sobriquet was "Swede," because of his fair skin, blond, wavy hair, and blue eyes. He was tall, lean, of Polish descent (2nd generation) and rarely smiled. I never knew him as well as I would have liked. But my Polish grandmother was the one I loved. She taught me much and helped to shape my character by teaching me honesty, hard work and integrity, all qualities that were reinforced by living in MacArthur's Japan. Somehow I knew then that I was different. Fortunately, I have not lived a life of "quiet desperation." Instead, I am well-educated, an environmentalist, gym rat, mercurial, and to some extent an iconoclast, refractory, a teacher and a caregiver to many humans and animals alike. While living in Japan my interest in history soared like a high-flying eagle. I was determined to make something of myself, even though I did not fit.

Prior to our departure to Ft. Lewis, I recall an incident with my Uncle George, a stocky Italian and a former Seabee with the United States Navy, who fought the Japanese in the Pacific theater. Uncle George hated "gooks" as he called them. The word "gook," a virulent form of racism, to be sure, originated, according to David Halberstam's *The Coldest Winter*, during the American suppression of Filipino rebels (1899). Simply put: It was American imperialism taking the Philippines from Spain, and attempting to civilize the little brown people as part of a Christian's duty regarding the White Man's Burden; Guerrillas were labeled "gugus" (or goo-goos) which eventually came out as an all-purpose name for Asians per se: "gooks." "Gugus" actually came from the bark of a local tree women used in their shampoo. The term "gook" has been used to identify and malign Asians in general.

Uncle George saw the bloody carnage. He gave me a knife, the handle crafted out of a dead Japanese soldier's bone. He did not want us going to Japan. Being very young, I simply buried the knife, feeling that this was the proper thing to do because of my sense of a Greater Being having created all living things.

At this time, my mother, brother and I were living in a ramshackle motel (Rodeo Court) in Colorado Springs. She worked as a waitress in the restaurant. We had cold cement flooring and two rooms. My mother hung red and white curtains and set down a gray, wool rug, which made it feel a little like a home. The window views were depressing. All one could see were other run-down, white, paint-chipped cottages needing big time refurbishing. Rodeo Court was desolation. One evening at sunset, I was an onlooker for a moment of horror. An internal natural gas explosion sent an entire collapsing stucco wall crashing downward and crushing my friend Larry's foot. The terror and image of his torment still echoes in my mind. I have no memory of the aftermath.

My private time consisted of listening to the radio and creating my own imaginary world with the voice of the "Lone Ranger," the "Green Hornet," "The Shadow," Arthur Godfrey, "Strike It Rich," "This is Your FBI," and many more. I also had to clean the place and care for my brother while my mother worked.

We had an open locker-room type shower without tile. Nothing but cold, rough cement flooring. Hot water was a luxury. More than once, I took showers with my mother to conserve hot water. I was mesmerized and aroused by her beautiful body.

My favorite time was nightfall. Like the artist Van Gogh, darkness created a certain comfort mood which blocked out much of the day. Also, like Van Gogh, I was a loner and felt alienated from family and friends. As a child, he ran away from home. I did likewise on one occasion. Art brought peace to his hostile world. Van Gogh's art expressed visual language in terms of color, line and composition.

Incidentally, latest scholarship suggests that Van Gogh did not commit suicide, but was shot in the stomach by a young boy from a distance.

My stepfather deployed to Japan in 1948. We were finally on our way in May of 1949 causing me to miss the final month of school.

The troop ship was pure fun. Movies, good chow, and the idea of crossing the Pacific Ocean thrilled me. Emotion overwhelmed President Ulysses Grant (1869-77) upon seeing the Pacific Ocean. He, in fact, was the first president to do so. I, likewise, experienced a similar sensation crossing the Pacific on my way to Japan in 1949. I did not mix with the other children. I kept to myself. We ate in the dining room off metal trays. Seconds were always available and it only cost a nickel for a Coke.

The old-fashioned 16mm movie projector was set among metal folding chairs. It groaned on as we saw many Westerns starring John Wayne, Wallace Beery, Alan Ladd, Gene Autry and Roy Rogers. John Wayne was my favorite all through my growing years, until recently. John Wayne is not the American icon I once thought because he dodged serving in World War II. Upon that discovery, my childhood cowboy hero is now to me a coward. Several stars who served stand out: Jimmy

Stewart, Clark Gable, James Arness, Lee Marvin, Audie Murphy, Jack Lemon and many others.

There were times that I worried when we hit rough weather. Sleeping was tough when the ship rocked back and forth. But I kept the faith with a Higher Power. Our bunk beds were narrow with hard springs and were uncomfortable because the mattresses were thin and lumpy. When rocking, I grabbed the sides out of fright.

On deck, I did see a whale from time to time amid the rolling waves and salt-water spray.

Truth
"The Smallest Atom of Truth Represents Some Man's Bitter Toil and Agony" – H. L. Mencken

III

Upon arriving in Yokohama in May of 1949, we were met by my father and proceeded by train to Camp Jinmachi on Honshu, more or less an outpost where the 7th Infantry Division was stationed.

The first year was enjoyable and exciting. We employed a gardener, houseboy and housegirl. They were lovely people. Our gardener, Kobayashi Gansobaro, was older and a veteran of the war. Photos of him and the other servants are still close to my heart. He was short in stature but long on character and honesty. His split-toed flip-flops always caught my attention as I had never seen such shoes. Additionally, I was fascinated watching him eat lunch out of his small, metal pail wrapped in a soft, blue cotton cloth. His expertise with chopsticks and sucking in each bite of white rice captured my attention. In addition to white boiled rice, he also ate fried grasshoppers (protein) and usually had certain berries topping his rice. He sat in our cramped boiler room near the side of our home. He never complained of my presence. The sushi component of his lunch forced me to look away as it was wrapped in cold eel and seaweed.

All three employees cost only chump change – even at that time. The gardener was a master constructor of a rabbit hutch, a duck pond, a fish pond with running water, and yes, a full garden of vegetables – all in my own backyard of the white duplex. Gardening, landscaping and flower arrangements are special in Japan. He was surprised when we did not fertilize the garden with human waste as was the custom in Japan at this time. Human waste was stored in "honey wells" collected in "honey buckets" and transported by horse-drawn "honey wagons" throughout the countryside. Japan's produce was beautiful, but off limits to Americans.

Our overall garden scene reflected a microcosmic picture of Japanese gardens. Our gardener used rocks, gravel and wood to create a small bridge over the duck pond. The garden did not have a bonsai which is usually a centerpiece in Japanese gardens. Some may call the bonsai a shrub because it is so short. The bonsai is meticulously manicured for generations. Roots and branches are regularly pruned along with root reduction, potting defoliation and grafting.

Our Japanese garden did resemble, to some extent, the Zen-style even though it did not display moving water; to the Japanese, moving water has a dynamic all of its own.

Speaking of water, Japan ranks in the top ten percent of countries with more than ample water resources whereas China and India will face serious water shortages in the near future. As a matter of record, Japan is selling water from its rich forest on the northernmost island of Hokkaido that maintains a famous ski resort and hot springs.

A Japanese stone lantern often appears at the entrance of Japanese gardens. The lantern is a welcoming symbol of grace to the visitor as are Japanese gardens in general, which create a sense of natural serenity and peace. We did not have a stone lantern.

I attended sixth grade at the Army Dependent School. It was fun and not like Catholic school. I made a few friends but still felt odd and out of place. By now, I had become a bit more rotund and was sometimes intimidated by a student who would swipe his pencil on the back of my shirts. I did nothing. Eventually, we divided up in so-called "gangs"—kids who were more like me versus the bullies. We had whips, chains and air rifles – until the military police collected our weapons and lectured our fathers, telling them to control their kids or repercussions would be forthcoming from military superiors. My dad busted my bottom for being involved. My gang was not really a gang but a bunch of kids who didn't like being pushed around. The military is always class-divided. Therefore, we who were children of enlisted personnel did not really associate with children whose fathers were officers.

During the school year, our teacher, Miss Taft, a tall, young, voluptuous strawberry blond with green eyes, prepared us for a play to be presented to the PTA. Her southern accent added to her mystique, along with her honey-tongued words. The play was about Kublai Khan and 13th Century China. The play's theme highlighted the Mongols' attempt to invade Japan (1274) and force them to surrender to Kublai Khan (who had conquered most of Asia in the 13th Century). As it was crossing the Sea of Japan, the Mongol fleet, fortunately for the Japanese, was diverted by a typhoon. This typhoon was called a "Divine Wind" or "Kamikaze," thus preventing the Chinese from landing on the west coast of Kyushu.

Militarists saw the "Divine Wind" as something akin to "Divine Invincibility" – thus believing that no harm would ever touch the Japanese home islands.

Much to their astonishment 16 B-25 Mitchell bombers launched from an aircraft carrier and led by General Jimmy Doolittle shattered this so-called "invincibility" in "The Doolittle Tokyo Raid" (April 1, 1942).

This first ever maneuver dropped numerous bombs on the Japanese homeland and sent a serious message to the Emperor: You are not "invincible" from the air. This event had a positive impact upon sagging American morale.

During World War II, Japanese suicide planes dive bombing on American naval ships were called "Kamikaze Pilots." Over 5,000 Japanese suicide bombers caused the greatest naval losses in United States naval history. Many of the pilots, moreover, did not believe the hype about the "divineness" of the mission. I share the empathetic insights of Kamikaze pilot Yasuo Kuwahara near the end of the book which makes this point.

Japanese suicide bombers are today still being glorified. Take the movie "I Go To Die For You," a nationalist film written by Tokyo's Governor Shintaro Ishihra paying homage to the past. Someone once said that nationalism is the measles of humankind. Then there is the photo wall with numerous Kamikaze pilots being admired at the Peace Museum for Kamikaze pilots in Chiran, Japan. This is a renewal of hero worship and the apotheosis of self-sacrifice which still predominates Japanese culture. Incidentally, according to *The New York Times International* (March 20, 2011, 12), Gov. Ishihara said "the earthquake and tsunami were divine punishment that should be used to sweep away the Japanese people's selfishness, materialism and worship of money." My take: American capitalism has ostensibly rubbed off on and corrupted Japan. The governor's comment is surely in contrast to their ancient culture and what I saw in MacArthur's orderly Japan.

During the class play, guess who was chosen to be the Khan? Yes, yours truly. I was to be costumed in a saffron-like robe and a horsehair mustache. Rehearsals went well.

PTA night arrived. We were set. The play began. Everyone was doing his part well – except for me. The horsehaired mustache tickled my nose. And I was simply too fat for the costume. At a certain juncture, I broke out laughing and popped my robe because of my fat tummy. The upshot was evident: I ruined the play. Miss Taft was irate, as she should have been. She apologized to the audience and once again I became a pariah. So, my first dramatic debut: a failure. I guess it was a good thing that my parents never attended one of my plays, sporting events or PTA meetings over the years.

Miss Taft never forgave me – and for good reason. On another occasion, I became entangled with her on Ski Hill, a huge, grass-covered knoll behind our school.

I always loved to climb it for exercise in summertime and sledding during the winter. So one sunny and warm Saturday afternoon, a friend and I took to climbing Ski Hill.   Upon arriving at the top, we encountered a partially dressed Miss Taft and a young Army officer in a certain embrace. We stared at each other briefly as she tried to cover up. They were engaged in the Jack and Jill syndrome but "they did not go up the hill to fetch a pail of water." I never lived this down either. I was happy when that school year was over but dreaded seeing her next fall. Because of a major historical event (the Korean War) I never again came in contact with Miss Taft, except in certain private fantasies.

Earthquakes are not foreign to Japan. Not at all. The first recorded natural disaster that struck Japan was the tsunami of A.D. 869. Then came the 1923 Tokyo quake that killed an estimated 140,000 people. Tokyo at this time was largely built of wood which led to massive fires.

The 1995 quake that hit Kobe took more than 6,400 lives, toppling an elevated expressway and wreaking havoc throughout the area. The 2011 9.0 magnitude quake was by far the worst of all. The repercussions will last for decades.

Mitsuko Watanabe, the 80-year-old owner of a small tobacco shop in the Tokyo neighborhood, pointed to the selfishness and untrustworthy politicians as causes of the devastation. And, according to Shinto beliefs, divine punishment is just punishment, something Mitze, our second housemaid, taught me while living in Sendai.

Miss Taft reminds me of the first American casualty in the 2011 tsunami. Miss Taylor Anderson, was a lovely 24-year-old teacher of English from Richmond, Virginia, who arrived in Ishinomaki, a small fishing and factory village just north of Sendai in 2008. She had a contract to teach English at eight schools through the Japan Exchange and Teaching Program. Anderson's diaries, with many entries, were found after the tsunami.

One diary indicated her desire to become fluent in Japanese, her love of Japanese culture, people and the country in general. In fact, she could manage 800 kanji Japanese characters which I was never able to do, even though I did learn a number of Japanese words during my youthful days in MacArthur's Japan.

Miss Taft was also involved in writing Japanese characters and exhibited a similar love of the Japanese people, culture and all. She often side-tracked her lectures with commentary on secular woodblock prints, for instance. She, as a matter of reference, had tickled my curiosity at the 6th grade level with her insight on culture, the arts and certain prints. I am positive, upon reflection, that she planted these thoughts which led me later in life to embrace Japanese prints. I did research on those prints, and they fascinated me. They were called *ukiyo-e prints*;

one print in particular called a "Winter Party" by Uthgawa Toyoharu, of the Edo Period in Japan, grabbed my attention. This scene involves three Geishas in kimonos entertaining two Japanese gentlemen—also in traditional dress; very colorful.

Ukiyo-e woodblock, black and white prints was an independent art form which had a special interest in townsman life. Woodblock gave the art a special character. Woodblock made *Ukiyo-e* unique and different from art forms—another contrast in Japanese life.

Woodcut prints often portray daily life, scenic vistas, actors and geishas. They also depict brightly decorative carp found in many Japanese gardens and, of course, the Emperor's moat in Tokyo.

Utamaro, Hiroshige and Hokusai are three of the most famous print artists.

One of Miss Taft's classroom walls was decorated with colorful paper of origami *cranes*, the Japanese symbol for longevity. Taylor Anderson's third grade students and Japanese friends distributed these beautiful paper origami *cranes* in her memory.

In a letter, the Japanese ambassador to the United States called Miss Anderson a "bridge between two nations." A true Venus in blue jeans. Her parents are struggling to make peace with their suffering.

This entire episode reminds me once again of the magic and beauty of Japan in contrast to the mayhem in their history.

Because my 6th grade teacher determined that I needed eyeglasses (she saw me squinting at the blackboard on many occasions), my father had to arrange a four-day leave to take me to Tokyo as Camp Jinmachi did not have a hospital or an EENT clinic, just a dispensary.

We boarded a Japanese train. Travel time was overnight—but slow compared to today's Shinkansen bullet train that tops 186 mph. Since my childhood days in Japan, I've always loved train travel. The "clack, clack" was music to my ears. It was hypnotic and soothing. Our military car was clean, quiet and comfortable as I recall, especially since it was 1950 and only five years after World War II.

While in Tokyo, we went sightseeing. It took two days to make the glasses which were G.I. issue, very plain, like vanilla. We also visited what I think was the Meiji Shrine, dedicated to the first Emperor of modern Japan. Asakusa is another historic area of Tokyo which we did not see; Asakusa is home to the oldest Buddhist temple.

Japanese Buddhism over time influenced my spiritual growth largely because it emphasizes reverence for the environment and all life.

Buddhism is not just for Buddhist monks; there are many practical aspects applicable for the layman as well. "The Four Noble Truths," for example, caught my eye. The "Truths" deal with the concept of human suffering in terms of its causes, the path to suffering, and finally the end of suffering through enlightenment. To a Buddhist, Nirvana is like blowing out a candle in one life, ready to light another in the next.

To me, Japanese Buddhism is more of a practical philosophy rather than a religion. Pragmatic philosophy guides one in life's choices. My family's second housegirl in Sendai was a Buddhist who spoke some English. We had numerous conversations about her beliefs.

Buddhism is rich and diverse. It taught me empathy, self-discipline, compassion and a warning to release my anger. Further, I learned that carrying grudges is wrong. My housegirl instructed me in meditation and deep breathing techniques. She used the analogy of allowing dirty bathwater to drain after pulling the plug in order to clear the mind through meditation.

Meditation causes one not to dwell on the past or future, leaving the mind a blank in the present, according to my dear friend Mitze. She also encouraged me to investigate yoga dealing with mantras such as Kundalini (Radiance) yoga that I now pursue.

Her influence upon my psychic still manifests itself from time to time. These mantras translated takes concentration on one's creative consciousness which moves one from darkness to light. The chants create abundant energy as well. Mitze reminded me that yoga and meditation would eventually take me to another place and bring truth to my identify.

Sitting cross-legged with hands clasped together in a praying sense, eyes closed, looking at the third eye and chanting **SAT NAM** many times manifests that truth. Another chant: **HAR HAR HAR** helps to create energy.

Japanese Buddhism can be compared to Humanistic Buddhism, a recent school that applies Buddhist core principles to daily life. It was founded in 1967 by Hsing Yun who was a refugee fleeing Mao Tse Tung's Communism in 1949. He established this brand of Buddhism at Fo Guang Shan Buddhist monastery set in the middle of a sprawling 55-acre bamboo forest on the island of Taiwan.

Those days of yore endured to the present in terms of the necessity to seriously address my anger issues which landed me in Anger Management School. I learned the difference between justified anger versus gratuitous rage or unjustified anger. I was fortunate later to find myself in a couple of seminars with Professor and former Tibetan Buddhist Robert Thurman of Columbia University, the father of actress Uma Thurman.

His powerful book, *Anger*, and lectures inspired me to extinguish the flames of my anger and dampen my flammable temper.

Dr. Thurman says that anger is fire linked to fear and, above all, to hurt, and to the anticipation of pain, which speaks to so much of my early life. He says further that anger kills happiness and creates suffering, which has been a blight on my life since those days in Japan and beyond. Maybe the hurt of not being adopted was a catalyst for my discomfort and a loss of control so many times.

Dr. Thurman taught me to realize that Buddhism would aid me in overcoming my anger by becoming a "knight of patience" (not one of my virtues, to be sure), to embrace tolerance, forgiveness, self-discipline and eventually gain wisdom.

He says that anger is a form of human suffering which is endemic in the world. Dr. Thurman says that today's global crisis is spurred by dogmatic ideologies, political corruption, religious fanaticism, social prejudice, poverty, a lack of wisdom, man's assault on the environment and most of all: Unruly voracity!

Finally, I add to that notion: capitalist greed, especially in the United States and the lack of gun control.

Firearms in Japan are essentially banned—except for shotguns, air rifles and those used in competition and research. My experience with an air rifle is sadly documented in this story.

Those who own said guns must endure a rigid background check, a mental and a physical test as well as regular government inspections. And yet, Japan is a thriving democracy without the equivalent of a superannuated Second Amendment. The Founding Fathers intended this amendment to protect people against standing armies.

In contrast, Americans own 35 to 50 percent of the worlds' civilian guns. Gun laws in the United States are the weakest in all the world due to the pressure of the National Rifle Association who dominate and own the pantyhose in Congress.

One wonders about President Lincoln's musing about "government by the people" in the Gettysburg Address (1863). The vast majority of the American people want a friendly version of gun control, including background checks, a ban on assault rifles and extra-long magazine clips. The NRA (founded in 1871 by former Union Army officers) oppose any form of gun safety control.

The M-16 type assault weapon can fire 2,000 rounds in a matter of minutes. This military assault rifle has no more place in a civil society than a M-1 Abrams tank.

The attempted murder of Rep Gabrielle Giffords (D-Ariz) in 2011 made no difference to the craven Congress.

In addition, the Sandy Hook killings failed to get the Congressional wimps' attention. To date, there have been in excess of 4,000 shootings since Sandy Hook.

The myopic NRA leadership says the Second Amendment is the basis for American freedom! Pure tommyrot! Great Britain, Canada, Australia and Japan—all enjoy freedom with strict gun control laws.

It is the First Amendment that guarantees American freedom—such as freedom of speech, religion, press, assembly and books—not guns.

The word "militia" noted in the Second Amendment—means "collective ownership"—not "individual." Past Supreme Court decisions document this interpretation. The Roberts Court has distorted the true meaning of the Second Amendment.

American government and judicial systems are corrupted by politicians without shame. It was Robert Penn Warren's great novel, *All the King's Men,* which best sums up American pols today: "{Pols} are conceived in sin and born into corruption and passeth from the stink of the didie to the stench of the Shroud." Gov. Willie Stark

In sum, says Rep. Debra Maggart (R-Tenn), a pro-gun NRA member, "If you don't do what{they} want {they} will annihilate you." (*The Washington Post*, A3, May 19, 2013)

Ricochet, by former NRA lobbyist Richard Feldman, gives an insider view of the dirty politics the NRA uses to bulldoze most members of Congress. It's a sledgehammer tactic that works: no meaningful gun legislation to date.

The NRA is a take-no-prisoner organization. No margin of error. Only one point of view tolerated! The NRA fails to realize that the Second Amendment is like all the other amendments: they are not absolute.

One afternoon around 4 p.m., my dad and I stopped outside the Dai Ichi Building to witness the end-of-day ceremony. The General walked down a short flight of cement steps and a carpet towards his awaiting military vehicle which would take him to the American Embassy where he, his family and four dogs lived. Pure pomp and circumstance! A small military band, honor guard and all the aura of a monarch greeted The General as a daily occurrence. I was awestruck and frozen in time. MacArthur was my idol. I knew then that all I ever wanted to be was a soldier. Years later after high school, I volunteered for military service while still a United States Army dependent, having lived the past two years in Austria and Germany.

The implausibility, of course, was after three days in a replacement depot in Frankfurt, Germany, I decided that I was on a fool's errand to think I was going to fit into the military mindset. No way! I had three years to think about it, though. But I did like being a member of the 82nd Airborne Division as a paramedic.

Today, Japan is one of America's staunchest allies and appointed its first female Minister of Defense, Yuriko Koike, now the former defense minister.

The postwar Constitution also contained Article 9 which effectively negated any thought of future Japanese armies being involved in combat actions. MacArthur literally forced the occupied government to accept this pacifist notion of renouncing war as a sovereign right – or even the threat of force as a means to resolve an international dispute. In addition, MacArthur compelled the Emperor to denounce political power and his God-like status. The Emperor becomes a mere symbol. In fact, the Emperor was really no more than a titular head prior to and during World War II. Why? Because he didn't rule, but, rather, reigned. The militarists ruled through Hirohito in the name of General Tojo.

The basic mission for the Japanese military since World War II has always been to defend the homeland. But this trend is in flux because the United States is bogged down in Afghanistan (like Vietnam). Ergo, the White House is calling for more Japanese boots on the ground.

Constitutional restrictions have prevented Japan from building aircraft carriers, but she has one of the best navies in the region. Japan has highly-regarded ground forces as well. Because of nationalistic fervor, Japanese politicians are urging Japan to take its rightful place on the world stage—contrary to the horrific atrocities committed during World War II. Despite Japan's dark historical past and recent nuclear and tsunami devastation, Japan's vitality is more than evident. Transportation is anything but slow, children are generally safe on the street, crime rate and unemployment are low. I witnessed this steely quality while living in MacArthur's Japan.

My recollection of this time is that the specter of militarism was still evident to a certain degree in that many of the ex-soldiers wore partial military garb and espoused a strong nationalistic sentiment regarding the Emperor who was technically a war criminal. As a youngster, I did not understand the notion of an Emperor being a war criminal and still allowed to reign as Emperor. But Hirohito was a war criminal. His order for United States airmen was simple: "Behead them." Blond and red-haired POW airmen were singled out for cruel punishment. They were often beaten and forced to work the Japanese coal mines with little food and water. But MacArthur realized that trying Hirohito as a war criminal would bring about chaos, anarchy and even guerrilla war tactics against the occupation forces.

Today, the 600 or more Japanese soldiers in Iraq are not permitted to use their weapons unless fired upon. In effect, the Self-Defense Forces (SDF) has not fired a shot or taken a life in combat in 60 years. MacArthur to the Japanese was like the Emperor, a deity. I did comprehend this concept.

General MacArthur's arrogance, aristocracy, egomania, sense of destiny, puffed up by vanity, flamboyance, self-confidence, insubordination, or simply put, his hubris suited him to become the quintessential military ruler of Japan (1945-51). He came by it all naturally according to William Manchester (*American Caesar*), as had his father, General Arthur MacArthur, similarly described by his contemporaries.

At age seventeen, Arthur MacArthur (1845-1912) joined the 24th Wisconsin Volunteers and gained his fame during the Civil War in 1863. He became an outstanding leader as he took the colors after the young color bearer was killed, shouting "On Wisconsin!" which today is the college fight song for the University of Wisconsin. He became one of the youngest officers in the Union Army and a Medal of Honor winner. Arthur MacArthur, otherwise known as "the boy Colonel," was a 3-star general upon his death. General MacArthur's father was instrumental in establishing the idea that an Army base should have a store, eventually called Post Exchange (PX).

My empathy and admiration for Douglas MacArthur has its roots in like-minded hubris, both positive and negative, depending on the beholder's eye. The conquered Japanese respected MacArthur's arrogance. Manchester said MacArthur was a man with a whip in hand who enjoyed every minute of it.

Unfortunately, this very trait, hubris, was The General's inevitable downfall, a classic Greek tragedy. General Douglas MacArthur believed most in General Douglas MacArthur. Even his second wife Jean called him "General" and not Doug. She did love him, according to her letters.

Douglas MacArthur was a born thespian. Dwight Eisenhower said he studied drama under MacArthur for nine years. Their disdain for each other was evident.

MacArthur believed he was a child of destiny. His image meant everything to him (as does mine). His corncob pipe was a mere prop as were his crushed scrambled egg hat and his constant sunglasses and pleated khaki trousers. He was vain. I understand vanity. Living in MacArthur's Japan reinforced my vain self-image as I emulated MacArthur's persona.

MacArthur's military trousers had to be pleated as were mine when I joined the 82nd Airborne Division. He hated neckties—unlike General George Patton, Jr., who during World War II required his troops to wear neckties even in combat.

MacArthur was moody and mercurial. While living in Japan, I received a number of punishments for a similar demeanor. Douglas MacArthur was remote and a loner; although on occasion he could exhibit irresistible charm. I've been accused of a similar personality trait by many misguided women.

MacArthur hated the expression "G.I.". He said, call them soldiers. Press stories were his *bete noire*. If The General did not like what he read, he sent the articles back for redaction and editing.

Douglas MacArthur had an extraordinary memory and knowledge of history, a man with a keen intellect. At West Point he scored higher than any other cadet in history. His entrance exam score was 100%. His grade average 98.17. No demerits, unlike U. S. Grant. West Point candidate Grant once received eight demerits for skipping church. MacArthur's love of history inspired me. I eventually earned two advanced degrees in history and became a history instructor.

MacArthur read voraciously. Plato, Napoleon, Mark Twain and Abraham Lincoln were his intellectual mentors. He also quoted Shakespeare and the Bible. Dostoevsky was his preferred author; *Crime and Punishment* his favorite book. The General was drawn to

Dostoevsky's psychological analysis of the inner feelings of the soul, how the intricate mind works and the notion of salvation and purification of the soul.

Russian history was a major area of study during my graduate studies at Georgetown University. I accompanied my Russian history students on two Russian excursions during the Cold War era.

Japanese culture taught honor and strict obedience to authority. This concept is dramatically evidenced by a Japanese lieutenant who held out in the Philippines from 1945 until 1974, never knowing that the war was over. He, like the entire Japanese Army, was drilled with the idea that surrender was verboten.

In fact, Japan had never surrendered in all of its history until August 1945. Even after two atomic bombs melted Hiroshima and Nagasaki, Japanese militarists were still not willing to give up. The "Warrior Code" did not permit surrender; surrender was tantamount to dishonor and disgrace. These militarists attempted a coup by taking the Emperor hostage in order to prevent him from speaking to the Japanese people in terms of unconditional surrender. President Truman, meanwhile, ordered the 315th Bomber Wing on a "final mission" against the Japanese homeland to reinforce the notion that one of the cruelest conflicts ever known to man was over. The most celebrated of the returning B-29s was the "Boomerang."

The "Boomerang's" crew had heard the surrender announcement while they were about 100 miles from their Guam home base. But they faced a serious dilemma: the fuel gage was flickering on "empty." Simply put, the last few miles were flown strictly on a "wing and a prayer." Fortunately, all 29 bombers made a safe landing.

About the same time, many of the Japanese militarists spilled their own blood. They honored the "Code of Bushido" by committing suicide, their ritual self-disembowelment. Seppuku in Japan is still the antidote to shame and failure; surrender, in fact, is synonymous with both shame and failure. Modern Japan has more than 30,000 suicides annually which make Japan a perennial leader in suicides among the industrialized so-called democracies. Their rate doubles that of the United States. Depressed young people account for most suicides. Reason: the stigma of failure, a major *cause celebre*. Anything from sleeping pill overdoses to sniffing detergent fumes to carbon monoxide poisoning is a factor in these deaths.

Since the 2011 earthquake and tsunami, the question is again begged: Will Japanese youth save the country?

The editors of *Time*, April 4, 2011, suggest that Japanese young people will "shame an ossified Establishment" and rally to roll up their sleeves.

Prior to the earthquake, far too many Japanese youngsters were described as "sociological neologisms;" in effect, *freeters*: young men and women who took low-paying and part-time jobs in order to avoid the responsibility of choosing a career, thus becoming underemployed, overindulged and pampered.

These adolescents were also referred to as *hikikomori*—youth who withdrew from society and life in general. Young males, for example, were more concerned with their appearance than their livelihood. They were looked upon as "parasite singles" who lived at home to avoid paying rent and supporting themselves.

Today, however, arising from the ashes, Japanese teens are saying: "What can we do?" They are volunteering in massive numbers to assist the elderly and earthquake victims in their daily needs such as bathing, dressing, finding food and shelter. They even volunteer to help those with no plumbing who have to relieve themselves in plastic bags, and then mix chemicals to harden the waste while covering the odor of fecal matter.

Taking daily life services for granted is a terrible mistake by us all. One only has to look back upon the Chernobyl disaster when a single reactor exploded killing many Russian workers and sent a massive cloud of cesium, plutonium and strontium across Belarus, Ukraine, Russia and Europe while a totally ineffective Russian government did little or nothing to mitigate this crisis.

Japan's renewal of sorts is being "blazed" by a youth movement despite a ten percent unemployment rate and one-third of college graduates with few if any job offers.

This youth surge is hampered, moreover, by a strangling red-tape bureaucracy and the likes of Tokyo Electric Power (Tepco), which failed to give survivors the raw truth about radiation and recovery time. Tepco says it will take "six to nine months" to end the nuclear crisis. What balderdash! Like most Japanese government dogma, this statement teems of the old "honey-bucket" days when I lived in MacArthur's Japan.

Philosopher and Nobel Prize winner for literature, Albert Camus, defined suicide as the only real important philosophical question in life. Camus said that life, after all, is meaningless and absurd. But despite the gloom, he likewise stated that one should still be able to find some happiness in life's inherent absurdity. A large segment of the Japanese people has yet to discover that element of happiness necessary to negate the cloud of failure that saturates Japanese society. From childhood, I also had been searching for happiness. Early life in Japan made me happy. Those halcyon days in MacArthur's Japan were nonpareil.

The two major religions of Japan are Buddhism and Shintoism and both are neutral on suicide, while Christianity considers suicide a sin. Shintoism being the indigenous religion teaches devotion to deities, reverence for ancestors and veneration of the Emperor as a god who was believed to be a descendant of the Sun Goddess. Confucianism's influence was minimal but nonetheless reflected a sense of "good behavior" and "order" on the Japanese people. The Japanese language evolved, in part, from Chinese characters. The only religion I knew at this time was Catholicism. My mother forced me to attend religious classes provided by the Catholic Chaplain. The only recollection I have is that the Chaplain constantly scratched his anus. I guess he had piles. I never completed the course because it did not resonate with my way of thinking.

I heard the story of the Emperor first-hand after arriving in Japan in the summer of 1949. During my short visit in Tokyo, I saw the Emperor's palace from the outside (through binoculars), located in the city's center. The grounds were immense. An algae-covered moat surrounded the palace grounds topped by a cement bridge. Toro lanterns, bamboo, cypress and pines hung over what my father called bonsai or two-hundred-year-old dwarf evergreen trees, all twisted in their joints. The moat symbolized the divide between mere mortals and the so-called divine Emperor; fishing the "divine carp" was a cause for beheading.

The Imperial palace was not much like the palace that I saw in movies. There were no sharp gables or stone wings, no tower or spires. As such, my dad said the place looked much like a combination of a wood and paper villa with sliding paper doors and very Oriental in appearance. But again, I was overwhelmed and felt lucky to see such an historical sight. To me, the view was jaw-dropping. Today, guided tours are conducted of the inner grounds.

Shakespeare said "Mercy is twice blessed." Today, unfortunately, there is no MacArthur "mercy" as such to offset Japan's worst economic and environment turmoil since my childhood days in Japan. Many retired Japanese used to go to Hawaii to play golf. Now they stay home and farm instead. Young people and older ones are rekindling their attachment to the land. As a matter of fact, Japan now produces 40 percent of the food they eat, thus boosting their self-sufficiency as a ripple effect of the economic downturn. Farmers no longer employ the "honey-bucket." Because of the 2011 earthquake, radiation from the nuclear power station will cripple Japan's agriculture for years to come.

Many dairy farmers dispose of most of their milk produced at their farm owing to the fear of radiation and contamination coming from the Fukushima Daiichi nuclear plant. The most severe radiation leak took place 48 hours after the hydrogen explosion at the Unit 2 reactor.

Prime Minister Nato Kan had given the situation total political spin saying that "there is a step-by-step improvement" despite the thousands of tons of contaminated water which flooded the buildings. To his credit, Kan created two Cabinet posts to oversee the nuclear crisis and tsunami reconstruction effort.

Best of all, Prime Minister Kan in a television address to the country said that Japan should decrease and eventually eliminate nuclear energy. Kan no longer believed in the "safety net" of nuclear energy. Here is an idea whose time has come for the United States to consider as well.

For a country still reeling from the worst nuclear disaster since WWII, 600 workers and engineers are building a new nuclear plant near the remote northwest town of Oma, a traditional fishing village.

The Fukushima meltdown contaminated more than 700 miles of land mass forcing some 50,000 people to abandon their homes.

Kan spoke of *Kizuna* which means he appreciates the "bonds of friendship" shown to Japan by the American public. Kan's emphasis was on the "geist" or spirit of the Japanese people arising from the ashes of World War II ("Japan's Road to Recovery and Rebirth," *The Washington Post*, Apr 17, 2011, A21). Kan failed to mention the MacArthur era's contribution as the key factor in Japan's remarkable recovery in the post-war period.

As a matter of record according to the World Bank, the average age of Japanese farmers is now 65. Agriculture represents only 1 to 2 percent of Japanese GDP.

Japanese farmers feel a sense of emergency because they cannot participate in free trade deals, unless the debt-saddled government infuses massive subsidies which it cannot afford, and the leaking radiation must cease.

Japanese homeless on welfare has reached 1.2 million so far, something unheard of since World War II, according to the *Asahi* newspaper and former Prime Minister Taro Aso. Since the 2011 earthquake, thousands more have become homeless and 28 thousand are still missing since the disruption.

The import-export shortfall, especially to the United States, has dropped close to 53 percent, a factor in the huge trade deficit with the U.S. The demand for Japanese autos and electronics has waned considerably. Sony, Pioneer, Nissan and Toshiba laid off thousands of contract workers. In my day, I saw very few Japanese autos except for the dirty, hot, charcoal-burning taxis in Tokyo. The 2011 tsunami has caused an auto parts shortage all around the world. Toyota Motor Corp. has curbed much of their auto-part output to Europe and North America. Toyota has been the world's largest car maker by volume.

Japan is seeking a new economic model. Until the 1980s, Japan relied heavily on export led-growth, namely the auto. Japan is noted for lower levels of imports, however. For every 120 autos exported to the U.S., Japan imported only one in comparison. Toyota Motor Company grew from a small spinoff in the 1930s to what it is today.

The yen was worth 425 to the dollar when I lived in Japan. It is now worth about 88 yen to the dollar. The yen rise is due to the dollar weakness. The Nikkei stock exchange has been at an all-time low as well. The 2011 earthquake and tsunami sent the stock exchange even lower. Stimulus packages similar to those in the United States have so far failed to right the sinking Japanese economy. An important question: Will the depressed climate and the notion of failure trigger an excess of suicides, typical of Japanese society as I remember postwar Japan?

Recent information indicates that Japanese businesses from auto makers to electronics are transferring much of their manufacturing goods abroad as the yen flirts with a new high against the dollar. In effect, Japan is restructuring its entire economy. More and more Japanese cars, for example, are being produced in Thailand.

Will party scandals that brought down the former Prime Minister Yukio Hatoyama continue to plague Japan? Will the safety troubles of the Toyota Motor Corporation impact the future of Japanese government? Will many Okinawans continue to object to the presence of rowdy U.S. Marines on the island—a primary reason for ending Hatoyama's reign as prime minister?

Current Japanese society reminds me of the turmoil I witnessed there as a child. In postwar Japan substandard living conditions, particularly in Northern Honshu, were ubiquitous which impacted my psyche forevermore. A similar environment existed in postwar Austria and Germany where I lived as a teenager, further exacerbating my pain. I recall Japanese people looking for food in refuse heaps whenever I roamed in villages and the countryside.

School day hectoring leads many to a feeling of failure, along with low-status jobs, all coterminous with failure. The end result is the emanation of the ancient "Code of Bushido" which still permeates Japanese society and culture. Prior to my journey to Japan, I was victimized by school bullies while attending first grade near Ft. Sill, Oklahoma. My first-grade teacher paraded me in front of the class as a paradigm of being neat and clean while lecturing other students that they should follow my example. Many of my classmates were Native Americans (Apaches) who were usually dirty, hungry, barefoot and poorly dressed.

My mother clothed me in white shorts, socks and shoes and curled my blond hair with a home permanent. After school I was beaten and rolled in the dirt. I ran home bloody, dirty and crying, until I fought back. From that time on, I stepped into my warrior persona, but I did not know it at the time.

I lived in postwar Japan on the northern section of the main island of Honshu at Camp Jinmachi, home of the 7th Infantry Division. (Japan is an island chain of four main islands: Hokkaido, Honshu, Shikoku and Kyushu) I felt an eerie sense of this "Code" because our gardener was a former Japanese soldier who still wore most of his uniform to work; he had a limited civilian wardrobe and he was proud of his service to the Emperor. I grew quite fond of this small man with a wide grin who spoke very little English but was able to communicate with me by way of gesture, facial expression and by drawings. He was an amiable and gentle man, very thankful for employment, the extra food and clothing provided to him and his family by my mother.

We also employed a dark-haired, young, tall house boy (boysan) and a short, young house girl (girlsan) with straight black hair who were able to speak some English. Through translation with the gardener, they told me how he fought Americans on Pacific islands. Upon hearing of the surrender, one of his buddies talked the gardener out of "hari-kari" (suicide).

Postwar Japan is regarded by most Americans as a lawfully structured society and a first-rate Asian ally. But according to reporter Jake Addelstein's book *Tokyo Vice: An American Reporter on the Police Beat in Japan*, Japan is ruled, in part, by underworld mobs, namely the Yakuza or Japanese Mafia. Addelstein, by the way, is under a constant death threat from the Yakuza because of his exposé on the mob. Jake lives in Tokyo with his family.

According to Addelstein, the Yakuza is not illegal in Japan. Mobsters wear their full-body tattoos and missing digits proudly. The Japanese Mafia follows the Samurai traditions. Full-body tattoos have a downside, however. They inhibit the body's sweating process, thus trapping body toxins which affect the liver.

A "60 Minutes" report indicated that a leading Yakuza Godfather made a deal with the FBI in order to enter the United States on a visa to receive a liver transplant. Why? Because the Japanese do not believe in transplanting organs. In return, this mobster was to "rat" on several Yakuza mobsters in the United States. The Godfather received his new liver in six weeks, well ahead of others who had waited for at least three years. When UCLA Medical Center was queried, they refused to be interviewed.

Further investigation by Addelstein revealed that the Mafia Godfather had "donated" over a million dollars to the UCLA unit. Additionally, two lesser mobsters who had accompanied their leader also received new livers – well ahead of others much higher on the transplant list. Again, no comment from UCLA.

The facetiousness: The FBI only recovered a mere pittance of information as promised by the Yakuza. Why, then, didn't the FBI demand this list up front – before the operation? As the cliché goes: "Money talks; BS walks."

Addelstein worries about being hit. The Yakuza offered him $500,000 to stop his reporting. Tempting, yes! But he said, "no deal." If Addelstein is "whacked" he knows that his body will end up buried in one of the tall buildings under construction, a Yakuza tradition.

Addelstein says that Yakuza comic books and fan magazines are sold in various convenience stores throughout Japan. He says further that mob bosses socialize regularly with the Prime Minister and politicians alike.

According to the National Police Agency (NPA) the Yakuza has about 80,000 members to date. Even the Osaka Securities Exchange and 50 other such companies are infested with mob parasites. To surmise that this does not affect the United States, think again; United States investors have invested billions in the Japanese stock market and essentially funding the Yakuza, at least, in part.

The Japanese judicial system does not have a RICO Act or employ plea-bargaining, witness protection or witness relocation programs. Therefore, the Japanese mob proliferates. But, the Japanese courts do not hesitate to deal harshly with flagrant crimes such as murder and rape. In 2008, for example, Japan hanged 13 convicted criminals – one being a notorious serial killer, Tsutomu Miyazaki, who murdered and raped four young girls in the 1980s, while leaving the charred remains of a four-year-old child on her parents' doorstep. He likewise made videotapes of the other mutilated corpses.

The former Prime Minister has ruled out any changes to the capital punishment policy, despite outcries from human rights groups such as Amnesty International, the European Union and certain G-8 members.

Modern Japan also does not have laws against owning child porn which enables Yakuza to make millions from this heinous, criminal enterprise. The Kabukicho neighborhood in Tokyo is a major red-light district which displays child porn in over 500 venues. My memories of Tokyo in 1950 are a little blurry but I do recall how crowded and dirty parts of the city were. I was aware of prostitutes and was curious as to what they did to survive postwar Japan. Teenage prostitutes are now available at any given moment. Certain retail stores even sell special undergarments worn by these child prostitutes. Worse, the Japanese government does not share intelligence regarding the Yakuza with United States government officials.

Again, living in postwar Japan, I encountered a number of "girly shows;" my buddy and I were curious adolescents, enthralled by nude photos displayed at various shops in certain villages that we visited looking for candy shops and, yes, bordellos, all off limits to American personnel, including dependents. My good friend and I did manage to sneak into some of these shows but were quickly discovered by a number of G.I.s who were also attending these off-limits events. Being a towheaded fat toad, I was most visible among the crowd of dark-haired Japanese who were all ethnically similar. My sidekick, David, by the way, was the Catholic chaplain's son who could speak some Japanese, thus opening many doors for us.

The "strip shows" were relief for a population struggling to survive day to day, all looking for a bowl of white rice, fried grasshoppers and a cup of Sake (rice wine) in addition to sexual gratification in some form. Japanese are quite open about sexual technique photos and the beauty of traditional Japanese entertainers called Geisha in full makeup and attire, wearing kimonos with rich colors and vibrant designs. They often strum a Shamisen, a stringed instrument looking a bit like a guitar. I once witnessed a lovely young woman in this garb, but being so young I was unable to appreciate the significance of what she represented. Nevertheless, I was all eyes upon her.

Japan and the rise of the Yakuza and other criminal activities are directly related to MacArthur's constitutional revolution, *ipso facto*, laying the foundation for a free and open society. Even today, Japan is the odd man out regarding negotiations with North Korea's nuclear program. The United States government has not included Japan in these talks.

Both Korea and Japan have serious political issues with each other. Korea kidnapped Japanese nationals in the 1970s and 1980s. Japan occupied Korea from 1910-1945. During World War II, thousands of Korean women were forced into sexual slavery by the Japanese army. However, during the occupation, Japan developed a network of roads, rail and postal services as well as telecommunications, hydroelectric plants, mines and some modern industrials, a typical Japanese paradox.

Japan has finally pledged billions to North Korea as reparation for the colonial occupation period. North Korea, meanwhile, has at least 300 or more medium-range missiles aimed at South Korea and Japan, thus not only endangering Japanese citizens but thousands of Americans as well. Reading such news today causes me to wish back when life was hard but very simple in old Japan.

Moreover, the potential of mass starvation is analogous to a Damoclean sword hanging over North Korea which may allow some negotiations; in essence, food in exchange for nukes. But Japan will not allow Korean ships in their ports which makes for a serious conundrum.

Another strain on modern Japan is the economic and military expansion of China. China, like Korea, also has serious World War II issues to settle with Japan who brutally raped China, especially Nanking. In this Age of Mobilization, China seeks markets for their slave-labor products which inundate the American economy, especially at Walmart.

Japan has invested well over 6 billion dollars in China and operates 20,000 or more companies there. And China has a huge appetite for Japanese technology and goods. Additionally, Japan sees more future markets in China than in the United States and Europe. By the same token, Japan does not want China to become the dominant Asian economic power and will in time do what it takes to thwart this dynamic. Japan and China are sparring over a chain of uncharted islands in the West China Sea, known to the Japanese as the Senaku and the Chinese as the Diaoyu islands. Japan seized these islands after defeating China in the Sino-Japanese conflict (1895).

At present, China is overtaking Japan as the world's second strongest economy. Remember this point: For hundreds of years, China was the greatest influence on Japanese culture which is based upon tribal, militaristic and clan traditions. Japan has borrowed heavily from the West to increase their power. In the 1930s, Japan became imperialistic and aggressive which led to the December 7, 1941, attack on the United States naval base at Pearl Harbor, thus triggering our involvement in World War II.

The aforementioned is a far cry from my early days in Japan. Despite the struggling economy in 1945-50, Japanese innovations were most visible. They used recycled American beer cans to fashion and market cheap trinkets, a precursor of the future Japanese economic juggernaut – the world's third largest economy which today is on life support, according to Wall Street.

What is not on life support is the fast food business also borrowed from the West. According to the *Economist* (July 17, 2010, p. 69), Bento lunch boxes have more than doubled; McDonald's has a six-year increase of sales – not to mention KFC's obscene profits.

There are consequences: Mothers cook fewer vegetables and sit-down dinners, while heart disease and cancer are on the rise, similar to the West.

Fast food production aside, Japan is the world's new gastronomic capital according to the *Wall Street Journal* (Oct 25, 2010, p. A-15).

Michelin, a 511-page all-world dining guide, gives its highest restaurant review to 12 eateries in Japan highlighting the cities of Osaka, Tokyo and Kobe. France is tops with 26 and New York with only 5.

According to *Michelin,* all *of* France's three-star ratings will shift to Japan in the future.

Japan will have the highest rated restaurants in the world, but that doesn't mean that they have better fare than France. Tokyo, for instance, has 160,000 eateries compared to 15,000 in Paris.

Tokyo is known for its international fare while Osaka is regarded as the culinary belly of Japan featuring everything from street vendors who sell "takoyaki," grilled balls of batter and octopus, as well as traditional "kaiseki" cuisine.

While living in Japan I never had a "yen" for Japanese nourishment, especially octopus or whale meat. It was not eupeptic in my mind. This scene reminds me of my adult visit to Denmark and being subjected to cooked eel which I simply turned down. On the matter of breaking bread, I cannot agree with Mark Twain who said: "…eat what you like and let the food fight it out inside."

A modern Tokyo vegetarian restaurant run by Aya Kakisawa, has on her menu sushi without fish. While I lived in old Japan, I never heard of such a dish. Her chef prepares a carrot "uni" (sea urchin) sushi made of kintoki carrots, a reddish carrot cultivated since the early years of Tokyo's existence known as the Edo Period.

Having been a vegetarian most of my adult life, I would still say, "No thank you." But there is one aspect of Japanese cooking that has been around for over 100 years and highly touted by American chefs as well. It is called *Umami,* "the fifth taste," a mainstream flavor in Japan tasting "savory" and "meaty." *Umami* is equated with a glutamate and is an amino acid derivative.

Japan's cuisine trumps the West in one major aspect: school lunches have become a source of national pride. In Japan, school lunches are a regular meal—made from scratch. Students eat in their classrooms and not in cafeterias as students do in American schools. Food is grown locally, never frozen and is Monsanto genetically modified free. And, there are no vending machines with junk food.

Umejma Elementary School in Tokyo is a model for the other 71 elementary and 37 middle schools.

As a student at the Sendai American School (1950-52) we always ate in a cafeteria setting. Every meal was hamburger, French fries or nitrate-filled hot dogs. Veggies were few and dessert was a sugar load. Japanese students are not allowed to bring a brown bag lunch, either.

The Element of Surprise
"All the Business of War...is to Find Out What You Do Know"
– The Duke of Wellington

IV

On a hot, early Sunday morning, June 25, 1950, 90,000 North Korean soldiers invaded the South, thus initiating the forgotten Korean War. Ironically, Korea is known as the "Land of the Morning Calm." The North Koreans capitalized on the element of surprise, thus overrunning South Korea and within three days seizing the capital of Seoul. Seoul was finally liberated on September 29, 1950, as a result of MacArthur's surprise Inchon Landing on September 15, 1950.

Because of the Korean war, the tenor of my young life changed dramatically along with so many others, both military and civilian, including the closing of our small dependent school at Camp Jinmachi and never again seeing Miss Taft.

As a young student of history, I followed with great interest the daily coverage of the Korean War published by the *Stars and Stripes*. The Korean climate and terrain were brutal, more so than Vietnam, especially the winter of 1950, the coldest ever. Colder, in fact, than the Battle of the Bulge during World War II.

I remember the very day the Korean War exploded. In Japan it was a blistery Sunday afternoon while I was at the Post swimming pool learning how to swim while swallowing gulps of chlorinated water. I was also wearing a white tee shirt to protect against being kissed by the sun while dog paddling and sinking to the bottom of the shallow end. The Korean War fascinated me and it needs to be viewed from the following perspectives:

-The Pusan Perimeter Break Out
-The Inchon Landing
-Pissing in the Yalu

- Frozen Chosin – MacArthur's Disaster "The Chosin Few"
- Chinese Intervention – Hell on Earth
- The all-black Army Ranger unit that made military history but never received a tribute for their service

On June 27, 1950, Truman issued his statement on Korea: "…I have ordered United States air and sea forces to give the Korean government troops cover and support…the attack upon Korea makes it plain…that Communism has passed beyond the use of subversion to conquer independent nations and will now use armed invasion and war.…"

Conservative pols led by Senator Robert Taft (R. Ohio) gave reluctant endorsement to the Truman decision on June 28, 1950. But Taft said that the possibility of this attack upon the South "…should have been foreseen by the administration…and by our intelligence forces.…" Taft was further concerned as to whether or not Truman was "…usurping his powers as Commander-in-Chief…because there has been no pretense of consulting Congress…there is no legal authority for what he had done."

Leon Trotsky once said that "you may not be interested in war, but war is interested in you." Thus, President Truman had no choice but to respond militarily. History says that presidents cannot pick the time the story begins—the story of war.

While back at the swimming pool, I heard the announcement on someone's portable radio. I toweled off and hailed a taxi jeep to rush me home, knowing that my dad would probably be deployed sooner than later. Taxi jeeps were driven by trusted Japanese nationals around the base as private automobiles were nearly non-existent. For a one-way trip around Camp Jinmachi one could travel for a five-cent Military Payment Certificate (MPC).

Upon arrival, my dad told me that he was "on alert." He expected the 7th Division to be sent to Korea very soon. I asked what would happen to my little brother, mother and myself. Would we be returned to the United States or what?

As an inquisitive 11 year old, I had no idea what I was going to face in the very near future. In addition to the *Stars and Stripes,* I slept ear-close to my cream-colored AM Arvin radio, tuned in to every Armed

Forces Radio (AFRS) broadcast that I could catch. I also attempted to listen to all the baseball games broadcast through AFRS, namely the Yankees' and Dodgers' rivalry.

Little did I know how disorganized and poorly trained United States troops were who were ordered to Korea from their bases in occupied Japan. MacArthur was the man of the hour and I wished that I were old enough to enlist and go to Korea. I envisioned being a platoon leader, leading a charge against North Koreans. A few weeks later I was shocked to hear that Major General Dean, commander of the 24th Infantry Division, had been captured. He was a Prisoner of War (POW) – a major general!

Had the general ever read Sun Tzu's *The Art of War*? Born at the time of Confucius (5th Cent. B.C.), Sun Tzu (meaning "Master Sun") had morphed from a warehouse manager into a world class philosopher. He evolved from a family and clan of arms experts, fighting experts and experts on strategy, espionage, deception and military tactics – all elucidated in his fighting manual, *The Art of War.*

This treatise on war teaches the power of deceit, psychology, strategy and tactics, and diplomacy as the essentials of war. History is replete with examples of Sun Tzu's fighting acumen. There were victories for those armies who embraced his teaching—and failure to those who disregarded Sun Tzu's guidelines. The American failure in the early phases of the Korean War can be attributed to Sun Tzu's admonitions.

Moreover, Vietnam, Iraq and Afghanistan likewise represent such failure, i.e., the idea of protracted wars almost always fail to achieve "victory." Then again, it depends on how one defines "victory." To wit: "There is no instance of a country having benefited from prolonged warfare." (*The Art of War*, Ch #11).

Furthermore, Sun Tzu said, "If you know neither the enemy nor yourself, you succumb in every battle." For openers, most troops into Korea and Vietnam could not find said countries on a map. Likewise, Iraq and Afghanistan to some degree. Worse yet, American soldiers going to the abovementioned countries knew or know little or nothing about the "culture"—a serious weakness.

The North Koreans, Chinese, Viet Cong and radical Muslims knew and know their enemy's mindset, thus following Sun Tzu's teachings: "Hence to fight and conquer…supreme excellence consists in breaking the enemy's resistance…."

The Tet Offensive in Vietnam (1968) is a prime example of a moral and psychological victory for the enemy. In Korea, a day after Thanksgiving, a 100,000 horde of screaming, bugling and whistle-blowing, drugged-up Chinese on opium, in tennis shoes, quilted uniforms and fur hats caught 10,000 First Marine Division Marines in their frozen sleeping bags at the Chosin Reservoir East near the Yalu River and well above the 38th Parallel—a so-called MacArthur screw-up during the brutal winter of 1950. The element of surprise caught MacArthur way off balance, a moral and military victory for the Chinese and North Koreans. But was it MacArthur's fault entirely?

First Marine Division General O.P. Smith was asked if he were retreating: his reply was simply, "Hell, no. We're attacking in another direction." An early 1950s movie was made of this historical event called "Retreat, Hell." I still remember this film version of the Chosin fighting.

It was 35 degrees below zero; wind chill made it 65 degrees below zero – cold enough to freeze eyeballs. One of the "Chosin Few," twenty-three-year-old Lt. Jerome McCabe, with frost-bitten, numb toes turned black, and a number of wounds to his arm and leg and bleeding from piercing shrapnel lacerations inflicted by Chinese border fire, crawled his way at least five miles to a group of friendlies who helped him to safety.

Chosin fighting is best described by historian Roy E. Appleman's *East of Chosin: Entrapment and Breakout in Korea* (1987). He says: "…the battles…soul-searching cold privation, exhaustion, heroism, sacrifice, leadership of high merit…but finally, unit and individual disaster." He continues: "…it would be hard to find a more…hopeless or more tragic story in American military history."

Chosin was frozen Hell! Jean Paul Sartre said "Hell is other people." Theologically, Hell is defined as a state of exile from the land of God.

James Joyce as a teenager was treated to the full version of Hell in terms of "being eaten with flames...goaded with burning spikes never to be free from the pains of Hell." (*The Economist* p.25 Dec 22, 2012)

For those frozen Marines, Chosin was all of the aforementioned.

Once the horrific fighting began on November 26, 1950, there were no more "warming tents." Prior to that time, Marines would be on line for two hours, then take a break in a "warming tent."

A sixty-year anniversary gathering was held at the U.S. Naval Memorial in Washington, D.C., on December 15, 2010, honoring the "Chosin Few." A superb documentary was followed by a panel discussion with a handful of the Chosin survivors. I was truly captivated by the entire evening and moved by the tears of sorrow flowing from a number of the veterans in the film and those present.

Sun Tzu speaks of "deception" as key to victory. Inchon was pure deception and brilliant. The Inchon Landing on September 15, 1950, was one of The General's greatest military feats. It was also a test of loyalty and faith to MacArthur. But his critics were numerous.

President Truman who considered MacArthur "a prima donna-brass hat," had sent the JCS to Tokyo to dissuade MacArthur. After all had spoken, MacArthur, with his corncob pipe in hand, said in a stentorian voice: "Gentlemen, I am going to Inchon in September and if I fail you will have a new commander." With that, he walked out of the room vainglorious and dignified. The JCS were humbled by The General. MacArthur was a mordant connoisseur of his own hubris.

The military objective was simple: to prevent United Nation forces from being driven off the Korean peninsula. MacArthur's inspiration for Inchon came from the Battle for Quebec (1759) during the French and Indian War. This was the final chapter in the struggle between the French and English for control of North America. British General Wolfe's troops scaled the cliffs of Quebec during the night (a near impossible task) to use the element of "surprise" to catch the French off guard. The British victory ended the French and Indian War and gave

England complete control of North America. To some it seemed like a pyrrhic victory because both Generals Wolfe and Montcalm lost their lives.

Because of high and low tides and navigating the treacherous water of Inchon Harbor, the odds for success were 5,000 to 1, according to MacArthur. High tides crested to 32 feet at 6:59 a.m and 7:19 p.m. At low tide the mud flats looked like deep, dark chocolate fudge. Unbeknownst to MacArthur and his aides was the fact that the Soviets had planned to mine Inchon Harbor but the train-car carrying the sea mines never arrived there in time.

I read every article in *Stars and Stripes* and listened to the broadcasts on AFRS radio regarding Inchon. My history teacher kept us informed as well.

The General's major supporter was Admiral James Doyle who believed in both the plan and MacArthur. Admiral Doyle worked out most of the details for MacArthur. During the planning stages, the Joint Chiefs were left out completely. MacArthur disliked the JCS, maybe even hated them. As history demonstrates, paybacks are hell: The Chiefs backed Truman 100% upon his decision to fire The General.

MacArthur loved the Navy because they rescued him from Corregidor during World War II as his troops were left behind. They suffered and died during the brutal and inhumane treatment by the Japanese during the Bataan Death March. But MacArthur had no choice. President Franklin D. Roosevelt ordered his evacuation to Australia.

In the main, Inchon tactics included taking three beaches, Green, Red and Blue, taking the city of Inchon, moving north to capture and hold Kimpo Airfield (essential to both sides), crossing the majestic Han River and finally liberating the capital city of Seoul.

By all measures, the Inchon Landing was a total success and MacArthur rewarded those who supported him and punished those who had no faith in the plan. MacArthur seemed invincible at this historical time.

The incredible "end-run" amphibious landing at Inchon turned the tide in the Korean conflict. As a matter of record, MacArthur, in

October of 1950, planned another such assault at Wonsan Harbor in order to rout retreating North Koreans. But the enemy had already departed. Historically, Wonsan was the last major amphibious landing attempt by the U.S. military.

Hindsight says that The General should have stopped after retaking Seoul and expanding the Pusan perimeter to the 38th Parallel. Did MacArthur receive advice to the contrary? Stay tuned! I was overjoyed at MacArthur's success and truly believed that the Korean War was over. Unfortunately, the war was far from over because of Chinese intervention. By December 1950, U.N. troops and thousands of refugees had to evacuate Inchon. Before retreating, American soldiers blew up existing fuel supplies that the North Koreans could have utilized.

Another happening during the Korean War that deserves mention but has been systematically left out of the historical coverage was about the first Army Rangers dropped behind enemy lines in March of 1951. This elite airborne Second Ranger Company served gallantly in Korea. For 60 years this unit, much like the Korean War, has been forgotten. Why? Because they were an all-black Army outfit.

The surviving members are today in their 80s. Finally, on Memorial Day 2011 in Washington, D.C., six former members were honored at the National Memorial Day Parade, while riding a float decorated with red, white and blue streamers. Nice, but too little too late!

Prior to landing in Korea, their ship docked in Hawaii for some needed R&R before facing combat. Upon entering a "dime-a-dance joint," they were told: "You guys can't go in there—only white soldiers." This was 1951—four years after President Truman by Executive Order issued an all-service integration because the racist Congress was unwilling. So much for American racism and the law.

In 1964, President Lyndon B. Johnson was given a de facto declaration of war against North Vietnam based on entirely false information as was George W. Bush regarding Iraq and weapons of mass destruction (WMD). These "deceptions" are usually backed by the military-industrial complex, not to mention the Eisenhower warnings at the end of his presidency. Arms merchants make a ton of money on war.

In Korea it was MacArthur's "no substitute for victory"—even to the extent of bringing on World War III with China to cover mistakes after the successful Inchon Landing by going past the 38th Parallel and "pissing in the Yalu" as did members of the First Cavalry Division. The 7th Cavalry was brevet General George Custer's regiment ("Custer's Last Stand" - June 1876) who saw most of the early fighting in the Korean War. They also witnessed the longest retreat south in American history. The 7th Cavalry's fighting song, "Gary Owen" was Custer's favorite:

> We are the pride of the Army
> And a regiment of great renown:
> Our name's on the pages of history
> *From sixty-six on down.*
> *We know no fear when stern duty*
> Calls us far away from home.
> It matters not where we're going
> Such you'll surely say as we march away, and
> Our band plays "Gary Owen."

MacArthur said he would use 50 atomic bombs against China. Mao Tse Tung's retort: "If you use atomic bombs, I will use hand grenades and still defeat you." European Allies were horrified, reminiscent of Hiroshima and Nagasaki.

MacArthur also signaled President Truman that he ran a better government in Japan than he did in Washington, D.C. The Cold War was now hot. MacArthur disgusted Truman. The President walked into a JCS meeting one day and said, "I'm going to fire the son-of-a-bitch." Truman now felt MacArthur breathing down his back as a political competitor.

Sun Tzu says nothing about using troops for nation building. Korea, Vietnam, Iraq and Afghanistan do not fit Sun Tzu's equation for victory and success.

During the early summer of 1950, after my father was deployed to Tokyo to train Republic of Korea (ROK) troops, my mother became deathly ill with spinal meningitis while pregnant with my sister. Meningitis (discovered in 1828) is the inflammation of the ménages that lie between the brain and skull. My mom had bacterial meningitis, which results in high fever, delirium, chills, nausea, and can cause permanent brain damage, paralysis, coma and death. This affliction moves quickly and needs to be treated within 24 hours. But there we were in a foreign country. Camp Jinmachi had only a dispensary and no hospital. The Korean War was raging and my father was far away. I was in a state of panic. Remember, I was only an eleven-year-old child fearing the death of my mother. She was so ill. I reached my neighbor next door who was the Post ice-cream maker sergeant-in-charge. Since there were only a skeleton number of troops on base, it was difficult to make contact with the right authorities.

My father was finally notified and he returned forthwith to our quarters at Camp Jinmachi. With a sense of dire urgency, my mother was taken by military ambulance to an awaiting aircraft and flown to Camp Sendai, about a hundred miles to the south where there was an Army hospital. My father accompanied her on this trip.

Before departing, he said to me in an ironclad voice and pointing with a minatory finger, "you are in charge until I return." Ever since that moment, I have always felt "in charge" and in control of my environment.

The tag "control freak" has followed me my entire adult life. Forlornness, futility and darkness were my perspectives. I was left to care for my six-year-old brother, along with our young Japanese maid. My dad gave her advanced payment and instructions. But she had to go home from time to time, which left us unattended during the black of night on many occasions. Most of all, apprehension haunted me.

Rumors were rampant. Possible World War III with the Russians and Chinese.

I often listened to my neighbor's short-wave radio. "Seoul City Sue" was a propagandist much like "Tokyo Rose" (World War II), "Hanoi Hannah" (Vietnam) and Axis Sally, an anti-Semitic American who was married to a Nazi and broadcast Nazi propaganda for Germany during World War II. Sally, upon her return to the U.S., served a 12-year prison sentence.

Tokyo Rose had been visiting her sick aunt in Japan when the war broke out. Militarists held her for propaganda value. She was born in California as Rose Tuguri, of Japanese-American parents who were now being herded into one of ten American concentration camps located in California, Utah, Arizona, Colorado and Montana.

A truly hideous sideshow of American history.

The militants forced her to broadcast propaganda and play American music. An effective propagandist, she was. After the war, Rose returned to the United States and was imprisoned for ten years. She served six and was pardoned by President Gerald Ford in 1977.

Without trial and with little or no warning, 120,000 Japanese-American citizens were evacuated (after Pearl Harbor) into internment camps enclosed by barbed wire and armed guards, mostly in sandy and hot desert country. They lived in tarpaper shelters surrounded by guard towers and machine guns. This sorry 1942 momentous occurrence was legalized by FDR's Executive Order #9066, sanctioned by the Supreme Court and strongly opposed by FBI Director J. Edgar Hoover. It was a well-kept secret that these prison camps were in construction—prior to Pearl Harbor, according to historian Greg Robinson, *A Tragedy of Democracy* and *By Order of the President*.

Meanwhile, many German-Americans were rounded up and relocated to a sanctuary in Crystal City, Texas, in rather comfortable housing with grass, trees, gardens, schools, swimming pools and other amenities. There were no tarpaper shacks, barbed wire or guard towers.

This shameful milestone was based upon West Coast racist hysteria and avidity. One Congressman said: "I'm for catching every Jap in America, Alaska and Hawaii now and putting them in concentration camps...Damn them! Let's get rid of them!" In today's vernacular, these words could be echoed by extremists in the Tea Party flock. FDR calmly signed the Executive Order. He didn't hate Japanese-Americans but he never felt them to be American citizens. He was, after all, a pol. And politics is a whore's game based upon lies. Three-fourths of these people were born of Japanese-American citizens (Nisei). The other fourth were

Issei—those born in Japan and not eligible for American citizenship. The prison camps endured for three years. All civil liberties were in the toilet. Most of these Japanese-Americans were entrepreneurs in the fruit and vegetable growing business. They not only lost their livelihoods but their homes as well, estimated at the time to be worth in excess of 100 million dollars.

Right-wing columnist Michelle Malkin puts a different spin on the internment process. Her book, *In Defense of Internment*, concludes that "the evacuation was a reasonable step taken under extreme pressure." She says further that perhaps 3,500 ethnic Japanese in America were active supporters of Japan's war effort. Malkin also states that at least 1,648 Japanese-American citizens fought with the Japanese Army and that over 5,000 Japanese-Americans renounced their citizenship in 1944 when the U.S. government allowed such an act. Personally, I don't believe a word of her fairy tale.

But it wasn't all negative. The camps provided something of a school system staffed by American administrators and teachers K-12. One of the best was Minidoka Japanese-American Relocation Center School located in Idaho. It was a part of the Densho: Japanese-American Legacy Project. The late Helen Manning worked at this relocation school. She taught 11th and 12th grade social studies, English and German.

At the outset in 1942, she and her students were housed in wooden barracks without curtains, desks or chalk boards. Later on, Miss Manning received some text books, chalk boards and desks that were bolted to the floor. As a result of her excellent teaching, most of her students graduated high school and attended a number of small colleges at the war's end in 1945.

Michi Weglyn's eyewitness account (*Years of Infamy*) documents the anger, misery, confusion, strikes, petitions, mass meetings and a refusal to sign loyalty oaths. Riots often occurred. These American citizens fought for their dignity and trashed constitutional rights. Not until the war ended did the American public learn of the concentration camps. A September 1945 *Harper's Magazine* article called the internment camps "our worst wartime mistake."

But was it a mistake? Not according to the late Professor Howard Zinn (*A People's History of the United States*) who says: "...an action to be expected from a nation with a long history of racism...a nation fighting a war not to end racism, but to retain the fundamental elements of the American system." World War II, according to Zinn, was a war to benefit the "wealthy elite" and the alliance between big business and government which has its roots in Alexander Hamilton and the Revolutionary War.

Vietnam, Iraq and Afghanistan continue the process. Three-fourths of military contracts in 1941 were stroked by 56 large American corporations. Has anything really changed?

Despite the patriotic zeal to win World War II, American workers were discontent. Well over 14,000 strikes happened involving six million laborers. Mines and steel mills were the hardest hit. It was Karl Marx, after all, who stated that the value of labor is determined by the worker. Poet Percy Bysshe Shelly supported this view; "There is no real wealth but the labor of man."

Professor Zinn sees the internment process as a "direct duplication of Fascism," one of the head-on threats to American democracy in 1941. The 1944 Supreme Court re-affirmed the relocation order in the case of *Korematsu v. United States*, stating that it was caused by a "military necessity." Finally, President Ronald Reagan decided that the survivors and descendents deserved some compensation for this Nazi-like roundup. In 1988, President Reagan signed a bill authorizing a $20,000 lump-sum payment to all survivors, along with an apology. Such a munificent gesture!

Columnist George F. Will has written that it is time for the Roberts Court to repudiate the 1944 *Konematsu* decision. (*The Washington Post*, A25, April 24, 2013) Will reports that the U.S. government hid from the previous Court a document prepared by the Chief of Naval Operations (1944) that 97 percent of Japanese-Americans were no problems and "...the Japanese problem...should be handled...{individually} and not on a racial basis."

Most of the anti-Asian racism in the 1930s and 40s was fueled by Earl Warren's rhetoric about the "Yellow Peril." He rode this rocket all the way to the Supreme Court's (1954) Chief Justice's chair.

The late William Hohri, born in San Francisco in 1927, was a leading advocate and plaintiff in a failed 25 billion dollar class action lawsuit against the federal government for damages. The 120,000 Japanese-Americans lost everything.

In 1942, Hohri and his mother were sent to Manzanar prison camp located at the foot of the Sierra Nevada. His father, a Methodist minister, was sent to Fort Missolia in Montana. While at Manzanar, Hohri completed high school and enrolled at the University of Chicago earning a Bachelor's Degree in religion and philosophy in 1949. Upon receiving his $20,000 stipend, Hohri purchased a new car, a Nissan; his custom license plate read: "REDRESS."

According to Captain James Bosworth, a former San Francisco journalist serving in Navy Intelligence at the time, said the Navy saw no military necessity for the internment. Only racism can begin to explain this tragic occurrence. One exception: Hawaii. Hawaiians trusted their Japanese. They were not imprisoned.

But, the U.S. military set down martial law in Hawaii. Civilian courts were replaced by military tribunals. Civil rights for Japanese-Americans were dashed. No due process for defendants. The U.S. Supreme Court finally stated that the U.S. Army rulings were unconstitutional. The Court said further that there was no evidence of Japanese-Americans colluding with the enemy.

This racist hysteria was not limited to the U.S. or Hawaii. Japanese-Canadians in British Columbia were likewise forced to evacuate.

A major U.S. newspaper, *The Denver Post*, supported the detention of innocent Americans while author Pearl Buck and Socialist Norman Thomas condemned the concentration camps.

And yet, the greatest irony: While many Japanese-American parents were in America's concentration camps, their sons were serving with the famous "Go for Broke" outfit known as the 442nd Regimental

Combat Team of the 100th Infantry Battalion. "Go for Broke" is a Hawaiian term for "shoot the works."

In November of 1944, the 442nd achieved their lasting fame by rescuing the "Lost Battalion," some 300 Texans of the 36th Division in France, who had been cut off from all support and surrounded by German soldiers. These Nazis held off all attempts to rescue the Texans for five weeks.

The 442nd at half strength took exactly thirty-five minutes to overrun the Germans and rescue the "Lost Battalion." The 442nd suffered 60% casualties—more KIAs than they rescued, in fact. After the war all members of the 442nd were made honorary Texas citizens. Big deal.

The 442nd was one of the most decorated units in American military history:

> 7 campaigns in Europe
> 7 Presidential Unit Citations
> 9,486 casualties
> 1 Medal of Honor
> 52 DCS's
> 560 Silver Stars
> 4,000 Bronze Stars

I read about this period of history while in Japan. I also remember my history teacher telling our class that greed may have played a part in this saga. He said that many of the Japanese-Americans were much better at farming, growing fruits and vegetables than the native California growers. Essentially, the Californian farmer wanted the Japanese-American farmer and their customers. This segment of history did not resonate with me until I graduated from college and began my own teaching career. During my first year of teaching history I included all the aspects of this story into my lesson plans.

I recall telling my class about one major ripple effect from the internment process: the precipitous decline of chick sexing. The science of chick sexing, that is, how to tell a rooster from a pullet, was dominated by Japanese-Americans (Nisei). They could turn out about 1200 chicks per hour as opposed to about 400 per hour by Caucasian chick sexers.

There came a howl from poultry farmers all over the United States as a result of 90% of the Nisei chick sexers in prison. It took about six months at chick sexing schools in Hattiesburg, Mississippi, and Tucker, Georgia, to turn out qualified chick sexers. The protest was so vehement that Uncle Sam eventually set free all camp qualified chick sexers. My former history teacher's admonition of greed finally hit home. The almighty dollar always takes precedence in American life.

Meanwhile, my mother's illness had to be attributed to our stay at the Japanese hotel in Tokyo. It was dirty and was run down. Since Tokyo had been firebombed on orders from General Curtis LeMay, much of the city still exposed the scars of this total and unnecessary destruction. About 100,000 people were burned to death. So the hotel was doing the best it could under these circumstances.

Currently, Tokyo hotels are very expensive, especially in the resort areas. During the 1950s, we did not know of any Japanese guest house known as "ryokanos," which are much cheaper than hotels. A "ryokano" today costs about $130 per night which is a deal compared to hotel prices. Our hostel cost in Tokyo was very low even for the 1950s.

In the past, "ryokanos" were traditional inns associated with resort areas only. That, of course, has changed in modern Japan.

The crucial happening for me at this hotel occurred when I decided to enter the spa or hot-bath area. Still learning how to swim fascinated me. One afternoon, I slipped into my bathing suit, grabbed my towel and walked to the lower level, anxious to enter the steaming water. I do not like cold water, so this suited me just fine. I became slightly embarrassed because my fat tummy overlapped the top of my suit. Upon arrival, I saw the Japanese attendant raising his hand, telling me to stop. Between his broken English and my limited Japanese, I figured out through hand gestures that I was to remove my bathing suit.

"Naked," I thought. "Oh, no!!" Stunned, I froze in place. "Do I really want to do this?" Since I was the only one there, I thought, "Oh, well, why not?" Unclad, I stepped into the murky hot water. After a few minutes of relaxation in water up to my chest, I felt safe—at least for the moment. Then my eyes rooted upon what was coming my way. There was mamasan, papasan, girlsan, and boysan all moving toward the entry steps. To my excitement, they were also in the buff. "Wow," I thought. For the life of me, I could not take my eyes off mamasan as she was no Jane Mansfield, but close. She bounced as she strolled; I could not stop staring. I wondered if she had what I would call today a "motorized" womb.

Now, I was in a dilemma. How was I going to exit without exposing myself? Banzi! (meaning "long life"). Suddenly, I turned my head and moved stealthily toward the steps, to my towel and then to the egress (P.T. Barnum used to charge 25 cents to "The Egress"). Ever since this experience, I am forever spellbound by ample female breasts, or as I called them in my youth: "big bazookas."

There were other memorable adventures in Tokyo. We traversed the Tokyo Ginza. I saw human-powered rickshaws all over the streets along with a fleet of bicycles. There were peddlers ad nauseum selling everything from cheap trinkets to smoked octopus. What really caught my attention were the Japanese coal-burning taxis.

Many of the open-air markets in Tokyo have been replaced with supermarkets and big box stores. The present-day open-air market runs under the elevated Yamanote Line between Ueno and Okachimachi Station. Venders galore hawk grilled squid to handbags much like the 1950 Tokyo I remember so well.

As a teenager while living in Germany, I often heard Tennessee Ernie Ford's "*16 Tons*." This song always reminds me of the coal-burning taxis. It also reminds me of American greed—the mania for the greenback dollar, even when that involves enslaving and exploiting men, and robbing them of their dignity and earnings with the "Company Store."

Loyalty
"Animals Are Such Agreeable Friends – They Ask No Questions, They Pass No Criticisms" – *Mr. Gilfil's Love Story*

V

While at Camp Jimnachi in the summer of 1950, I felt abandoned with my brother while mother was hospitalized and father remained in Tokyo preparing for deployment to Korea. Dependents left behind had to practice air-raid drills, often at night. We had jerry-rigged air-raid shelters near our quarters, simply large foxholes with a top. The idea of having to run to these holes in the middle of the night nearly terrorized me. When darkness fell, I became despondent, yearning for my parents.

In early August of 1950, I received word that my mother survived and I had a new baby sister as well. Best of all, my dad had been reassigned to Camp Sendai with the Japan Logistical Command (JLC). My brother and I would be relocating at some point to Camp Sendai, an expansive base with all the refinements provided by the United States Army for its dependents, including a new school.

I learned that dad was returning soon. Upon his arrival, my brother and I were joyous. Dad said it would be a few weeks before the transfer took effect. He averred that we would be settled in time for school. All of a sudden, the pending transition from Jinmachi to Sendai reminded me of a Biblical truth: "the light that dawns in the darkness."

I now felt mature beyond my years—even though I still maintained a devilish streak in my living soul. Case in point: My dad left his travel bag open one day. Being inquisitive, I examined the contents. Much to my surprise, I discovered a pack of condoms. Reserving judgment, I knew that most United States soldiers solicited Japanese prostitutes; my father was no exception. He soon told me that he had to return to Sendai to visit my recovering mother and baby sister. Additionally, he said he must report to his new commander and secure our living quarters.

Unfortunately for me, he left his loaded .45 caliber holstered pistol attached to an olive drab Army issue pistol belt tucked away under a towel in the linen closet. Being a John Wayne fan, I envisioned myself donning a gun around my waist like a gunslinger. After he departed, I removed the gun and adjusted the pistol belt to my fat waist. For the next day or so, I strutted around the house with my pistol.

At certain times, I would unholster the weapon in order to "draw" then point it at the maid, making her bow. She obliged but would rattle Japanese and broken English my way. She raised her hands, then bowed. Now, I was a real cowboy, so I thought. In addition to the maid, I told my brother to dance when I pointed the pistol at him. He did, but wailed mournfully.

Then my dad returned from Camp Sendai. The maid and my brother could not wait to tell him what I had done. Well, did I catch a lake of fire! He took a belt and beat me on the backside until my welts bled. Feeling defiant, I did not cry, regardless of the cruel pain. I looked up at him and said, "Is that the best you've got?" ("The tongue can no man tame; it is an unruly evil." James 3:8) Since he never adopted me, I felt at that time, my impudent behavior was justified.

Remaining days at Camp Jinmachi were psychologically dark, dreary and joyless. After my justified belt thwacking, I realized the potential danger and angst that I had caused the Japanese maid and frightened brother, their comfort level and mine were destroyed.

After this incident, my irate father, with his stern visage rarely spoke, except to give me orders. But he did make sure we had enough food and other essentials. The neighbor lady (ice-cream sergeant's wife) checked on us regularly and kept us supplied with ice cream. I opened many soup packages and made a lot of peanut butter and jelly sandwiches.

The August heat bothered me, especially at nightfall. No air conditioning or fans. These nights reminded me of a yesteryear while living in Lawton, Oklahoma. Sweltering summer night heat caused me to select the coolness of the porcelain bathtub for sleeping.

During the month of August, dad split time between Camp Jinmachi and Camp Sendai, spending his non-duty hours with my mother and baby sister who was named "Ginger," short for Virginia. Both mother and sister survived the dreaded meningitis affliction, as far as I knew. Kudos go to the Army doctors who treated them. Later on as the years passed, I realized mother suffered some minor brain damage due to the high fever associated with her infirmity. She was never quite the same.

Dad, the maid and houseboy began packing our belongings to be shipped to Sendai. The red, mud-flapped, balloon-tire Schwinn bicycle was my most treasured possession. I took pride in washing, waxing and oiling my bike and rode many miles around Camp Jinmachi.

Because of the solitary days awaiting the outcome of my mother's malady and growing danger of the Korean War, I found soda pop, candy and ice cream comforting to my choppy emotions. It was Oscar Wilde who said: "The advantage of emotions is that they lead you astray."

A few days after dad departed to Sendai, I witnessed a 24-hour period of near hysteria. Jinmachi caught the tail end of a monster typhoon. The earsplitting wind reminded me of the mournful howl of a baying wolf. Window panes rattled and nearly burst. At any moment, I believed the roof would be torn away. White knuckle and gut-wrenching fear dominated me. I resorted to prayer: "Prayer is and remains always a native and deepest impulse of the soul of man." (Thomas Carlyle)

The absence of light and a quaking house startled me. Little brother cried. I maintained order despite the impending danger. But fear and danger just creates more danger. Controlling emotions amid flickering candle light was not easy.

Having suffered through the storm by early dawn, I ran to the backyard to check on my pet white rabbits. The toppled and damaged hutch caused my heart to sink. They were all dead. Tears flowed like a rushing waterfall. My love of animals lightened my burden and helped me to quiet my fears; above all, they reinforced my spirit. Now the rabbits were gone.

A few years before arriving in Japan, a beautiful, black, curly-haired dog named Dinky had saved my life by literally pulling me off a major highway after I had tripped over my own feet while crossing.

Since my early bond with animals in general and dogs in particular, I was so affected by Japan's most famous statue: A dog named Hachiko. This dog exemplifies duty, perseverance and loyalty—all qualities Japanese. Hachiko met his owner upon his return from work each and every afternoon at the train station.

One day, unfortunately, the owner passed away at work; but Hachiko faithfully arrived at the same spot for the next ten years until he died in 1935.

Nicholas D. Kristof of *The New York Times* and once of the Tokyo Bureau, wishes that some day Japan will erect a similar monument to the loyal nuclear plant workers who likewise epitomize those same qualities of duty, dedication, stoicism and discipline regarding the failed nuclear plant destroyed by the 2011 earthquake and tsunami.

Kristof also mentions the fact that the only "looters" after the tragedy were not Japanese—but foreigners.

Since post-war Japan, my heart-bond with animals was forever forged like a steel weld. ("We can judge the heart of man by his treatment of animals." I. Kant)

As an adult looking back on my life in Japan, I am tormented by the beauty of Japanese culture and the character qualities previously mentioned, against the violence of World War II and the wanton killing of whales, dolphins and sharks.

Yet, to erect the statue of a loyal dog touches me deeply which is congruent with Japanese Buddhism that teaches reverence for all life.

MacArthur to Ridgeway
"Duty is Like a Man's Shadow; it Follows Wherever You Go" –
Marcus Aurelius

VI

Arrival at Camp Sendai was uplifting. Seeing our new digs, a detached, white three-bedroom bungalow located next door to the Post swimming pool excited me. To think I could walk out my front or back door in my bathing suit was just dandy. Then came the rapture of seeing my mother and sister; thinking we are a family, at least for now, warmed my heart. At this point, I thought my mother's near-death experience may have saved my dad's life as his new assignment with the JLC meant that the killing fields of Korea were not in the cards for him.

It was 1951 and the Korean War raged on. As a rising 7th grader, my historical curiosity intensified. Knowing that school bells would soon ring, I wanted to be ahead of my fellow students regarding current events.

My radio tuned to AFRS ran overtime nightly and I grabbed a daily *Stars and Stripes*, devouring every word about the Korean War. I did not totally comprehend the coverage, but I made the effort to understand the anti-Communist mood in the United States driving a liberal-conservative consensus in terms of President Truman's undeclared war in Korea, an ongoing oft-told narrative in the news.

Japan occupied Korea for thirty-five years. After World War II, the 38th Parallel divided the two countries. Syngman Rhee, the South Korean dictator, was not popular with many Washington, D.C. politicians because of his dictatorial policies.

But the same politicians remember Secretary of State Dean Acheson's 1949 National Press Club speech indicating that Korea was not on the radar of the Asian Defense Perimeter—the green light for North Korean dictator Kim ll-sung to invade the South with Stalin's permission, of course.

At 4 a.m. Korean time on June 25, 1950, the North Korean flood gates opened. In Washington, it was 3 p.m. on Saturday. President Truman was at his home in Independence, Missouri. Secretary of State Dean Acheson was at his Maryland farm. At 6:30 a.m. Korean time, President Rhee realized that his country was being overrun.

Miscalculations during early phases of the war made it difficult for MacArthur's forces to react. Kim ll-sung believed that the South would rise up and join his legions. Sygman Rhee, a Christian, Princeton graduate and a friend of Woodrow Wilson, wanted to unite all of Korea under his rule. It is a wonder that Rhee was a friend as Wilson had a racist range of vision.

One wonders how the South Korean dictator S. Rhee, General MacArthur and President Truman would have reacted to the massive artillery strike launched by the North Koreans using Soviet-made SA-2 surface-to-air missiles on South Korean soil, namely, Yeonpyeong Island, occupied by 1700 South Koreans. The Island lies in the Yellow Sea 72 miles west of Seoul and 7 miles from North Korea.

General MacArthur never had an interest in Korea. American occupation troops in Japan, under his command, were lazy, undisciplined, poorly trained and equipped. I saw this first hand as my dad often took me to his outfit.

The United States State Department fared no better. Some believed MacArthur was too old at 70 and suffering from Parkinson's disease. His hands shook while receiving the unconditional surrender document aboard the Battleship Missouri anchored in Tokyo Bay on September 2, 1945.

John Muccio, United States Ambassador to South Korea, had sent MacArthur warnings and advice of a possible incursion by the North. He paid little attention to the danger. Jonathan Swift's insight revealed: "How is it possible to expect mankind to take advice when they will not…take warning?"

MacArthur reacted slowly to the aggression. On that very night he watched a movie after dinner as he did most evenings. The General suffered from mood swings. Rules that applied to others did not apply to MacArthur.

Back at Independence, Missouri, Truman's thoughts reflected upon the 1938 Munich appeasement conference when Western democracies failed to thwart Hitler. Truman's mantra reflected Jeffersonian principles:

- Question with boldness
- Hold to the truth
- Speak without fear

Historically, Truman is the best read of all presidents, despite the fact that he had no college degree.

Truman also thought about Churchill's 1947 "Iron Curtain Speech" at Fulton, Missouri, and George Kennan's 1947 *Foreign Affairs* article regarding containment of Soviet Communism. Thus, Truman decided on a "Police Action" to send United States troops to Korea to contain Communism while choosing General Douglas MacArthur as his Supreme Commander—against, I might add, warnings from retired General Dwight Eisenhower.

Ike wanted to see paratrooper General Mathew Ridgeway of World War II fame take the Command. Ike told Truman that MacArthur was too old and untouchable. He schooled Truman on MacArthur's brutal actions involving the forced removal of the Bonus Marchers from Washington, D.C. in 1932, all veterans of World War I who only wanted what was coming to them. This was the time of the Great Depression. President Hoover simply turned a deaf ear to the burning of tents and Gestapo-like tactics employed by MacArthur, George Patton, Jr. and others.

Ike called MacArthur a "dumb son-of-a-bitch" by the way he handled the Bonus Marchers. At the end of World War II, Eisenhower maintained over 200 concentration camps in Germany near the end of victory in Europe (V-E Day), 1945. Over one million German POWs and civilians suffered in heat and snow without shelters, little or no food or medical care. Most died a horrible death. Ike hated Germans. In a letter to his wife he said they "were beasts who must be punished." He even hated his own name. General George Patton, Jr. allowed his German POWs to escape rather than send them to Ike's camps. Patton called these prisons "Gestapo-like."

This history is well documented in two books by author and historian James Bacque (*Other Losses* – Little Brown). FDR knew of these concentration camps as did Churchill, Charles DeGaulle and others like FDR's son who was in on the initial meetings. France maintained several more camps. In fact, many Germans were still prisoners and forced to fight against General Giap and Ho Chi Minh's troops at Dien Bien Phu (Indo-China) in 1954. As a teenager living in post-war Austria, Germany, I met two survivors of these camps.

The *New York Times* ran editorials supporting General MacArthur's appointment as commander, saying he is the "best man; that fate could not have chosen a better man." MacArthur's devotees felt that God was only senior to MacArthur.

According to David Halberstam, The General was surrounded by a "staff of sycophantics." He names General Almond (MacArthur's Chief of Staff) as the leading sycophant. General Almond said MacArthur was the "greatest man on earth." Almond made light of rumors about the possibility of Chinese intervention. In fact, he said American soldiers should not worry about Chinese "laundermen" as any kind of threat. But General Stilwell of China fame said MacArthur had been a general too long and that he lived in an insolated world since receiving his first star in 1918. MacArthur, a self-proclaimed prophet, took no prisoners, did not listen to advice and only listened to what he wanted to hear. He was the first to receive the Purple Heart Medal for his wounds in World War I.

During their service in the Philippines, MacArthur said Eisenhower was the best clerk he ever had. President Truman never had any love for MacArthur. As early as 1948, he wanted to recall The General. But that would kill Truman politically. Anti-Semites and racists supported MacArthur to a large extent. The Truman-MacArthur political tug of war culminated on Wake Island in October 1950.

Camp Sendai (Kawauchi Tract) was a Metropolis compared to Camp Jinmachi. It was a sprawling base with a five-year-old school established in 1947 (K-12), a well-run snack bar where a cheeseburger cost 50 cents, a movie theater, great gymnasium, baseball, softball and football fields, a large swimming pool, a dandy teenage club, modern military housing, a consumer-oriented Post Exchange and the 172nd Station Hospital located in Sendai City. This medical facility saved my mother's life and this is where my baby sister was born.

Camp Sendai was also the home of the IX Corps and the JLC. As a seventh and eighth-grade history student and keen follower of the Korean War, the Wake Island meeting between The General and President Truman interested me.

Sendai American Dependent School employed a well-informed and educated faculty, especially my history teacher, Mr. Austin Tucker, from Nashville, Tennessee, and a graduate of Peabody College. He also coached our basketball team, high school and junior varsity or middle school team of which I was a member.

Mr. Tucker used the Korean War as current events and history. He stressed the constitutional idea that MacArthur was pressing his luck with Truman when The General failed to salute his commander-in-chief upon deplaning at Wake Island. Truman irritated MacArthur by asking him to meet there – their first person-to-person encounter. According to history, Mr. Truman was later asked if he had noticed that General MacArthur failed to salute him. Mr. Truman's reply: "You're Goddamned right I noticed!"

The President and The General stepped into the back seat of a military vehicle that took them to the conference site. On the way, Truman admonished MacArthur, saying I am the commander-in-chief and you are The General. At the base movie theater, the newsreels played up the Truman-MacArthur split.

Mr. Tucker's stirring lectures emphasized the fact that the United States military is always under civilian control, so decreed by the United States Constitution. By December 1950, the Chiefs turned on The General because of Chinese intervention and a losing military situation. They were Janus-faced, in my view.

The Chiefs emphasized the fact that MacArthur's major duty was to maintain the safety of Japan and they were against committing additional troops believing that a major war should not be fought in Korea because of the risk of a global conflict involving Red China and the Soviet Union.

It was General Omar Bradley's (JCS head) testimony during the Senate hearings who after Chinese interventions said: "Red China is not the powerful nation seeking to dominate the world…in the opinion of the Joint Chiefs of Staff, [MacArthur's] strategy would involve us in the wrong war, at the wrong place, at the wrong time and with the wrong enemy."

Bradley's speech before the Senate basically destroyed MacArthur's argument for attacking the sanctuaries in Red China. Bradley wanted to oppose Communist aggression in Korea without provoking a world war.

MacArthur's response to the JCS view was rather blunt: "That is not war—that is appeasement. We could blockade the coast of China; destroy…China's industrial capacity to wage war; …release…the Formosan garrison…if we are forced to evacuate Korea without taking military measures against China…it would have the most adverse effect upon…Asia, not excepting the Japanese…."

By March of 1951, UN troops had regained lost territory back to the 38th Parallel. Truman now wanted a cease fire and a settlement to the Korean War. MacArthur disagreed. He was supported by House Republican Leader Joseph W. Martin, Jr: "Your admirers are legion, and the respect you command is enormous…." MacArthur's reply to Martin: "As you pointed out, we must win. There is no substitute for victory."

As a seasoned historian, I found data to prove that MacArthur was misled by the Joint Chiefs, by the White House, by the Pentagon and by Dean Acheson, Secretary of State, regarding his order to cross the 38th Parallel.

While MacArthur was winning, he was more or less given *carte blanche* with regard to Korea, particularly after the very successful Inchon

Landing in September of 1950. After Inchon, MacArthur felt invincible which speaks to his insolence at Wake Island. Manchester feels that MacArthur was never told exactly what was expected of him.

At the Wake Conference, MacArthur assured President Truman that the boys would be coming home by Christmas and that the Chinese would never enter the Korean War. MacArthur told Truman that if the Chinese did enter, "the Yalu will run red with Chinese blood." But as history knows, on November 26, 1950, 250,000 Chinese troops (about nine divisions) charged the Marines at the frozen Chosin Reservoir near the Yalu and Chinese border.

Former Secretary of State George Marshall (1947-49), famous for the Marshall Plan which prevented Western Europe from being overrun by Communism after World War II, sent MacArthur a cable saying that the White House wanted him to feel "unhampered" both tactically and strategically to proceed north past the 38th Parallel. (Manchester, *American Caesar*)

Incidentally, the Marshall Plan included tons of tobacco products as part of the aid. For every two dollars, one was earmarked for Virginia tobacco. As a child, to me every Japanese smoked American cigarettes purchased on the Black Market.

MacArthur responded: "I regard all Korea as open for our military operations." (Manchester, *American Caesar*)

Soviet historian and diplomat George Kennan (father of the Containment Policy, vis-à-vis the Soviet Union) told Dean Acheson that moving ahead of the 38th Parallel was not a good idea and this would rankle the Soviets.

Was MacArthur, then, given a "green light" by the Joint Chiefs as well? They told MacArthur to "plan for the possible occupation of North Korea." (Manchester, *American Caesar*)

Churchill's best known World War II military leader, General Montgomery, said that generals are rarely given adequate directives. The Chiefs also told MacArthur to "go ahead and conduct military operations north of the 38th Parallel." MacArthur at this point had serious reservations about his orders, as did Truman.

The result is that MacArthur was beguiled and victimized by the JCS, Secretary of Defense, the State Department and the President of the United States himself. Truman said he went along because of what MacArthur had told him at Wake Island. A pitiful excuse. Truth be told: No one in Washington wanted to know that the Chinese had been infiltrating since early October. Those that entered were referred to as "Coolies," or "volunteers."

The Chinese tried to settle the Korean question prior to their intervention. Mao's foreign minister, Chou En-lai, sent word to the United Nations concerning Korea and a possible solution—before MacArthur crossed the 38th Parallel. Again, Dean Acheson convinced Truman that MacArthuur should cross the 38th Parallel.

Was MacArthur supposed to read the minds of the dictators in Peking and Moscow? Why didn't the United Nations Security Council interject warnings about the Chinese? Truth of the matter: American diplomats disregarded the Chinese threats as a simple bluff. A wily diplomat can tell you to go to hell in such a way that you actually enjoy the trip. Korea was now floundering. It was Churchill who said, "War is a catalogue of blunders."

The confused cauldron of diplomacy boiled over. On April 11, 1951, General Douglas MacArthur was fired—or in diplomatic parlance, "recalled."

I witnessed this entire day in history when 250,000 weeping Japanese were in long lines waving Japanese and American flags. Japanese people lost their savior. MacArthur—a scapegoat for failure—was succeeded by the paratroop general of World War II fame, General Mathew B. Ridgeway, who dramatically changed the botched course of the Korean War.

Truman added: "In the simplest terms…we are trying to prevent a third world war…if we were to bomb Manchuria and China…we would be running a…grave risk of starting a general war…. If that were to happen, we would have brought about the exact situation we are trying to prevent. …I have, therefore, considered it essential to relieve General MacArthur."

On April 19, 1951, MacArthur delivered his magniloquent farewell address with éclat to a joint session of Congress: "...the Communist threat is a global one...you cannot appeace or...surrender to Communism in Asia without...undermining...efforts to halt its advance in Europe...I know war as few other men now living know it...War's very object is victory—not prolonged indecision. In war...there can be no substitute for victory...appeasement... begets new and bloodier war.... I am closing my 52 years of military service...the world has turned over many times since I took the oath on the plain at West Point...I still remember the refrain of one of the most popular barrack ballads of that day...'Old soldiers never die; they just fade away.' And like that old soldier. I just fade away—an old soldier who tried to do his duty as God gave him the light to see that duty. Good-bye." A congressional standing ovation followed. Then a confetti-covered parade down New York's Fifth Avenue, thanking The General. Truman's riposte: "Pure bullshit."

The old soldier never faded away in Norfolk, Virginia. There is an eight-foot statue of his likeness (like the one at West Point) outside his memorial and Visitor's Center, a three-building complex amid the charm of a tree-lined square where The General and his second wife Jean, lie in state.

Poet Joyce Kilmer ("Trees"), like MacArthur, was known for reckless bravery during World War I (1918) at the Battle of the Marne. Kilmer served with The General when he was a colonel; MacArthur eventually becoming the commanding general of the 42nd Rainbow Division named by him because of its members coming from all walks of life.

Kilmer lost his life while MacArthur was recommend for the Medal of Honor and a Purple Heart.

The Visitor's Center houses the Chrysler Crown Imperial The General used during the occupation of Japan. As a child on a visit to Tokyo, I saw MacArthur in an olive drab military vehicle, only.

Outside the Center is a memorial garden in honor of the thousands imprisoned in Japanese death camps.

President Truman appointed General Matthew Bunker Ridgeway as Supreme Commander, Allied Power in the Far East, upon the Presidential firing of General Douglas MacArthur.

Ridgeway took a broken and beaten Eighth Army to new heights. The previous commander of the Eighth, General Walton Walker, had been killed in a jeep accident. Under Walker, the Eighth was known as the "bug-out" Eighth. MacArthur had treated Walker with disdain.

Once the Eighth had been driven to the Pusan Perimeter, my history teacher feared a possible invasion of Japan. I thought it was a stretch or overreaction because life at Camp Sendai was so comfortable and Shangri-La-like.

Korea seemed, on the one hand, so far away to me. On the other, I felt very close to the action as I kept a constant vigil on the radio (AFRS reports) and read avidly the ongoing *Stars and Stripes* articles covering the war. MacArthur was still the leading man. I hated his dismissal because I did not fully understand the constitutional issue that well. I felt it was personal.

But now, my focus was on General Ridgeway. His photo ops in the *Stars and Stripes* pictured him with two grenades hanging on a parachute harness, jump wings attached to his chest and a mention of his mirror-like paratroop boots. As of the first photos of Ridgeway, I decided then and there that I was going to join the Army and become a paratrooper in the 82nd Airborne Division like General Ridgeway. During World War II, General Ridgeway had succeeded General Omar Bradley, the first commander of the 82nd—after it had become an airborne division.

That childhood dream became reality in May of 1957 as I became a member of the 82nd Airborne Division, stationed at Fort Bragg, North Carolina, where I attended Jump School and earned my blood wings, so-called graduation lead-colored wings. After graduation, I was proud to wear silver jump wings, the famous 82nd shoulder patch and the "DEVILS IN BAGGY PANTS" insignia. Best of all, I excelled in wearing dark Cordovan and highly spit-shined jump boots. Fellow troopers often paid me to shine their boots prior to our inspections, and I loved wearing tailored and pleated uniforms.

When my history teacher assigned us written reports concerning some aspect of the Korean War, I chose to research the evolution of the 82nd Division and General Ridgeway. The Post library was more than adequate with many books on military history, a given, of course, on an Army base in a foreign country.

I discovered that the 82nd was an Infantry division during World War I. It is called the All-American Division because its members come from every state in the Union. And much to my pleasant surprise, I learned that a famous celebrity soldier had served with the 82nd in France during World War I. His name: Sergeant Alvin York, Medal of Honor winner. I remembered the story of Sergeant York from the 1941 movie starring Gary Cooper. But the 82nd notion did not register with me at that time. Sergeant York won the Medal of Honor because he single-handedly shot 20 German soldiers, took out 35 machine guns and captured 132 German POWs. As a child, I was impressed by this historical data.

Research took me further into the Ridgeway story. General Ridgeway, prior to shipping out with the 82nd Airborne during World War II, had invited Sergeant York to speak to his troops. He held Ridgeway's troops in awe, especially after they heard why he was a Medal of Honor winner. York told Ridgeway's troops to be aggressive, be well-trained, be fully armed and learn to be an expert marksman between 20 to 50 yards. As a result, Ridgeway built an efficient firing range which included woods and difficult terrain. His 82nd troopers were ready to fight Nazi Germans. It would be a "Schnitzel" takedown.

In Korea, General Ridgeway turned an almost defeat into an eventual truce and stalemate in 1953. His fighting Eighth drove the Red Chinese out of South Korea. The rabble Eighth was no longer. According to Clay Blair (*Ridgeway's Paratroopers*), "...Ridgeway arrived on the battlefield with an unflinching determination to turn defeat into victory, disaster into triumph." The Eighth Army had just received a rib-cracking embrace from General Ridgeway.

Chairman of the Joint Chiefs, General Omar Bradley said, "It is not often…that a single battlefield commander can make a decisive difference…. In Korea, Ridgeway proved to be the exception. His brilliant driving leadership…turned the tide…like no other general in our history."

Life at Camp Sendai: Mr. Tucker's History Class
"Education Makes People Easy to Lead, But Difficult to Drive, Easy to Govern, But Impossible to Enslave" – Baron Brougham, 1778-1868

VII

Back at Kawauchi Tract (Camp Sendai) my school was in full operation upon my arrival in 1950. Prior to this time, the school was conducted through correspondence courses administered through the University of Nebraska. The school at Sendai was designed to accommodate 250 students and completed in 1947. The academy re-opened in September 1948. During my time, the school graduated 12 students and eventually had a total enrollment of 465 students.

The school hierarchy consisted of the Regional Post Commander, Colonel John Taylor DeCamp, whose son Billy was a senior at the time. Billy was chubby and wore braces, but was an outstanding basketball player. I was fond of him, admiring his athletic and leadership skills. At one point he arranged a job for me at the Post movie theater. I always worked for my money, even as a child. No allowances. All movies were free to me and I received a princely sum for my services as a ticket taker. Since Billy's father was Post commander, Billy had clout. For me, this was a good deal.

As I reflect upon my yearbook (*The Samurai*), I am moved by many heartfelt memories of so long ago. By the same token I never forgot that mother was ill and recovering from a life-threatening situation. Nor did I neglect to spend a lot of time helping with baby sister.

My school principal was cool—that is, Mr. Victor V. Cool, a graduate of Kansas State College with a B.S. in Science and a Masters in Physics. He was popular with fellow Japanese administrators who dropped in on our classes numerous times. In return, we likewise visited many Japanese learning centers during the academic year. Mr. Cool was amiable and fair. I cannot recall any negatives about him, and that is a rarity since I spent 32 years as an educator myself. I encountered so many weak administrators who didn't know a noun from an aardvark.

The School Board consisted of six people: three military, two captains and a sergeant. Mr. Cool, Mrs. Beaubien and Mrs. Tate completed the package. Captain Beaubien was also the School Liaison Officer. An effective structure, to be sure.

From a young child's perspective, Japan was scenic with bamboo, pines, mountains and many thatched roof villages. It was an adventurous time. Simply fascinating!

When we were on a field trip to visit Japanese schools, the children often greeted us with overt politeness, bows, gaiety and simplicity. Their buildings resembled papier-mâché construction, and were very flimsy. Doors, for example, between classrooms were paper thin. I do not remember seeing a lot of wood. After all, the time was only six years or so after World War II. Wood was scarce. Japanese schools in 1951 were quite primitive.

They were eager to learn English and I was anxious to learn Japanese.

Japanese students looked small and doll-like to me. Upon meeting them, they tried their best to say "hallo;" upon leaving they would say "goo-by."

The first words I learned in Japanese included:

"Moshi, Moshi, Anonay?" (Hello, Hello, Are you there?)
"Dozo" (please)
"Ha" (yes)
"Ah so desuka" (is that so)
"Domo arigato" (thank you)
"Sayonara" (goodbye)
"Ano" (pardon me)
"Sake" (rice wine)

In addition, I learned how to count 1-10, to say "good morning," "good evening," and some words that I shall not repeat here.

Times have changed since then. In 1989, for example, students at Great Falls Elementary School in Fairfax County, Virginia, created the first Japanese immersion program in the American public school system. These young people have been learning science, math and other basic subjects in Japanese and they even dress in traditional Japanese garb at times.

This program has impressed Japanese elites such as the Emperor, Empress and a series of ambassadors who actually visited the school in 1996.

Further, each year sixth graders spend a week in Japan where they are greeted by the top leaders, as a symbol of binational friendship between the United States and Japan. (*The Washington Post.* Oct 17, 2010, p. C3*)*

MacArthur's Japan was upbeat. That is because of The General's skillful handling of the occupation—despite the hard-liners (militants) who wanted Hirohito to never surrender and rally behind their cry: "Drive out the Barbarians!"

On one occasion, the militarists were disturbed after a photo appeared (shortly after the unconditional surrender) of the Emperor holding his black silk top hat standing next to the much taller MacArthur in front of the American Embassy. Many Japanese thought the photo was a fake and the Emperor was forced to submit. Not the case. It was Hirohito's idea via his Foreign Minister Shigeru Yoshida, who had informed The General of the Emperor's request.

The General could not set foot in the palace of a conquered foe, nor could he ask the Emperor to call on him at the public Dai Ichi Building. Simply stated, this would humiliate Hirohito. That is why the American Embassy was the proper meeting place. Saving face was crucial for both egos.

MacArthur spoke to Hirohito through an interpreter. Out of respect, The General wore khaki, no rank, no insignia or decorations. The Emperor was attired in striped black trousers and a claw-hammer coat. His translator was called "Kido the Clock," a diminutive figure in his fifties who was a time perfectionist, to the atomic second (no pun intended).

Approaching The General made Hirohito nervous. His hands shook. MacArthur offered him an American cigarette which he gladly accepted saying "thank you" in Japanese. Historically, the Russians and British wanted MacArthur to indict the Emperor as a war criminal. MacArthur knew better as previously explained. Maintaining the dignity of the Emperor was the key to a stable occupation society. MacArthur also had empathy of one aristocrat to another.

Manchester wrote this about MacArthur's thinking at the time: "…it is painful to see a man {Hirohito} so high and mighty brought down so low."

After the meeting, Hirohito published a poem in a Tokyo newspaper to allay the concerns of his people:

> "The pine is brave
> That changes not its color,
> Bearing the snow,
> People, too
> Like it should be"

I recall my teacher of English, Miss Anna Freeman, from Worthington, Ohio, reading the poem from the blackboard to our class. She said that the "snow" represented the American Army occupying Japan and the "people" were the brave Japanese and for them not to change their character because of the "snow." Saving face, she said, was so important to people who had never historically surrendered until now. Made sense to me, even as a 7th grader. I wistfully imagined the mental picture.

From that time on, The General and Emperor met twice yearly; some historians felt they had developed a father-son type relationship. It was MacArthur's respective approach with the Emperor that created a "spiritual regeneration" of Japan, according to Manchester. Many Japanese eventually felt that it was because of MacArthur's dignified demeanor toward the Emperor which made the occupation so stellar. In spite of MacArthur's hubris and prima donna status, he did warn the

American press not to make heroes out of generals and admirals and to stop glorifying war. As a history instructor for over 30 years, I admire MacArthur's warning because America has engaged in wars of aggression in Vietnam (1965), Iraq (2003) and in the past: the Mexican War (1845, we stole Texas fair and square), the Spanish-American War (of Manifest Destiny, 1898), and we had no business in World War I (1917) bailing out British bankers and setting the stage for World War II.

A prophecy came forth in April of 1967 by Martin Luther King, Jr., in one of the greatest speeches of conscience in the 20th century entitled: "Beyond Vietnam." He said Vietnam was a lie and "destroying the soul of America" —that he could no longer be silent as "Silence Betrays Truth," his mantra and message. He would no doubt say the same today of Iraq and Afghanistan, both politically corrupt.

Life at Camp Sendai seemed thoroughly American. It was home away from home unless I went off base, as I did many times. I really didn't feel the foreign-land aspect very much. It was difficult to think of the Japanese people in terms of Pearl Harbor and the horrible atrocities of the Bataan Death March. Bataan was known before the Japanese takeover as "the Pearl of the Orient," a true paradise.

General MacArthur had been sent to the Philippines to fix a broken ragtag Filipino army. As the Japanese were invading the Philippines, FDR ordered MacArthur to Australia, leaving behind his American Army and General Wainwright. The epithet "Doug Out Doug" came about as a result of this event. Japanese cruelty on the Bataan Death March (1942) can never be forgotten or forgiven. Never! Why? Because the Japanese government to this day has never shown contrition or acknowledged their war crimes, particularly the Bataan Death March.

A ten-day, 60-mile march killed several thousand Americans who were deprived of food, water and even denied the humane concern for bathroom necessities. They reached Camp O'Donnell, a garrison started by Americans but never completed. There were 55,000 POWs who survived the ordeal. The camp was inadequate with little or no water, food or sanitary latrines. As many as 60 suffering Americans died daily while

450 Filipinos died on a quotidian basis for a total of 26,000 by the time of liberation. During the incarceration, a number of American POWs actually stole food from fellow prisoners. That is incredible desperation.

Many American POWs were sent from the POW camp to Japanese Hell Ships taking these emaciated and sick human beings to the coal mines in Japan.

Primary source material and eye-witness accounts indicate that once in the mines, life was pure hell. Since most Americans are taller than the Japanese, the American POWs were forced to work for hours in a bent-over position. And those with red or blond hair and blue eyes were brutalized even more so.

Meanwhile, back at the POW camp, Americans were divided into 10-man teams. If one escaped or attempted to escape, the remainder would have to dig their own graves, then kneel before the pit, bend over while their hands were tied behind their backs, and a Japanese soldier with a Samurai lopped off the head of each man. Others had to watch the heads roll into the grave and if anyone closed their eyes or turned their heads, they were also beheaded.

The late Mildred Dalton Manning was held captive along with 77 other military nurses in Manila's Santo Thomas prison camp for three years (1942-45). She was the last known female POW of WWII who died in 2013 at the age of 98. She and others labored as nurses at the outdoor makeshift clinic on Baatan.

Her daily ration consisted of two bowls of watery and bug-infested white rice. She, like the rest of the POWs, suffered beriberi and dengue fever in addition to malnutrition but still managed to nurse the sick.

The weak and emaciated POWs were finally rescued in February 1945 by a U.S. tank battalion. Breaking out, the POWs erupted into "God Bless America."

Yet upon liberation and homecoming, the "Battling Bastards of Bataan," were once again left behind. Most suffered from serious mental issues. They were not afforded help. Today, America celebrates Pearl Harbor Day. But what about Bataan Day? It doesn't exist!

At the time (1951), I did not know exactly how to deal with the history of Bataan. My history teacher told us prior to his lectures that this material would be difficult to process. He had a special interest in this story, for he knew one of the survivors. This teacher's honesty about history left a major imprint on my psyche.

The hired Japanese nationals at Camp Sendai were friendly and accommodating. Our housemaid (only one this time) worked very hard for little pay. Her Japanese name was "Mitshe." We called her "Mitzy" for short. She was older and educated to a certain degree but did not like working for Americans as she felt housework and babysitting were beneath her. Luckily, she liked me for whatever reason. As an eighth grader, I found her views on Buddhism interesting and meaningful.

My school engaged a Japanese custodial staff. I remember "Harry" (Koresumi Tacahoshi), Nariko and Hanacho who did an excellent job maintaining our edifice. I never forgot Nariko's bobby sox and black and white shoes that were purchased at the base PX.

Camp Sendai had a lively teenage club which played '50s music on a regular basis. There were Rosemary Clooney's "Come on-a my House," "This Old House," Eddy Arnold's "I'll Hold You in My Heart," "Bouquet of Roses," "Cattle Call," and so many more. Also, Patti Page's "Tennessee Waltz" and "Doggie in the Window," Nat King Cole's "Mona Lisa," Johnnie Ray's "Cry," Jo Stafford's "You Belong to Me," and on it went. A true cornucopia of great music.

Being a "wall-flower," I usually sat in a corner wishing otherwise. I did have a crush on a girl a few years older by the name of Loraine Nordling, who was from Los Angeles, California. But I never had the grit to speak up.

Thereafter, because of my bashfulness, I decided that I needed to break out of my introversion. I started going to the Post gym, daring to play basketball, lifting weights, and losing some of my belly fat. Guess what? I've been a gym rat ever since, wherever I landed. The gym has always been my second home to this very day.

Since mother was weak, I helped the housemaid with cleaning and caring for both my brother and sister whenever possible. My sister was young. I took her with me to different places on the base. She could walk a little, very cute with curly brown hair and a sweet face. At one point, I entered her in the Post baby contest—and won! I was so proud and thrilled. We bonded at a very early age.

Once the basketball season began, I tried out for the junior high team. Since I had spent so much time in practice, I had acquired some basic skills, but I was still a bit clumsy and awkward at times. My movements were not elegantly kinetic.

Mr. Tucker, our coach, arranged for us to play age-appropriate Japanese teams. Looking back at *The Samurai* yearbook, I see myself larger than anyone on the court but among the less skilled players. The smaller Japanese boys were so quick and agile. They were motivated to beat Americans and we wanted to defeat them as well. Being sizable, strong and aggressive, I used my body weight and bulk to advantage at times to rebound and score a few points, not to mention throwing an elbow on occasion.

We had a .500 season. And it was fun. I was called a number of times for over- aggressive play. That has matched my living body ever since, aggressive and persistent, yet still shy especially when it comes to girls, even though I've always been fascinated by the female anatomy, and a long-term admirer of feminine pulchritude. At one time, my father confiscated my wallet and discovered what we call today porno pics of Japanese women in all kinds of situations. I remember grabbing them from his hand and running out of the house. I did not return for a number of hours, totally embarrassed. Upon my reappearance, he did not belittle me but warned that I was way too young to get involved—that it could ruin my health. I took his advice to heart and never dated for many years until I was 18 years old and a senior in high school. I met a beautiful young lady in Germany in the '50s when she was 14 (and married her years later). My story is much like the Elvis Presley courtship of Priscilla whom he met in Germany in the '50s when she was only 14 (and later married). Another similarity with Elvis: I also had a twin brother who died at birth. Likewise, I was also in the Army in Germany in the 1950s, as was Elvis.

Considering that the war with Japan had only ended in 1945, the United States government provided a plethora of amenities for American dependents by 1950-51.

Besides excellent living quarters, there were post exchanges, movie theaters, hospitals, gymnasiums, ball fields, snack bars, NCO and Officers' Clubs and, of course, American schools staffed with the best of personnel. As young dependents, we had teenage clubs, access to swimming pools as well as tours to the many historic sights still standing in certain areas of Japan.

Amid all of the positives, there were many Japanese who were still suffering from the effects of radiation, a very poor economy and the overall aftershock of such a terrible war. All the while, the Korean War continued to rage and American soldiers were dying due to a poorly executed war – that is, until General Ridgeway took over the command ship.

Meanwhile, our American school offered all the basic courses to K-12, including many athletic activities. Best of all was the basketball program coached by Mr. Tucker.

In 1951, eight boys turned out for the high school squad. They all made the team. The season was set up to have league and non-league play followed by a tournament at the end of the season (Nov-Feb) in Tokyo where all the high schools would compete. Non-league games included competition between the high schoolers and United States military teams as well as Japanese high school squads. My junior high team only played against Japanese junior high schoolers.

Our high school season totaled 29 games and compiled a won-lost record of 9-20 plus two losses at the tournament. But they had a great time! The Osaka trip, for example, was extended in order for the team and cheerleaders to visit the second largest city in Japan and the famous Osaka Castle.

As a player, I learned much about sportsmanship, controlling my temper to some extent and was determined thereafter to practice the basics and perfect shooting skills and team play. Most of all, I was so impressed by the agility of these very young and smallish Japanese kids and their ability to communicate and move with such élan.

My being large and clumsy was a bit of an embarrassment. From that time on, my gym-rat days had begun.

There was one military team which could have competed with some of the squads of today at a similar level. That was the 50th Signal Battalion which started two semi-pro players creating much excitement for all of us who were fans.

They eventually won the Post championship. Sadly, many of them lost their lives in the "land of the morning calm."

As a high school athlete in later years while living in Austria and Germany, I traveled over much of Europe to compete in sporting events including football, basketball and track. Once I even participated in the music festival even though I was a member of the "off-key club." Like the days in Japan, all dependent players were given per diem money as well as taxpayer accommodations and transportation.

Other sporting events at Sendai included a volleyball team and a summer softball squad. My debut as a catcher reminded me of my first dramatic performance one year earlier: a total failure. I was too young and unskilled to catch high school fast balls. But I gave it a try, although I was afraid of being hit by the batter.

As stated earlier, I did leave the base on a number of occasions, some out of necessity and others out of curiosity with my friend, David. We traversed Sendai City and the outskirts many times. On one trip to Sendai City we distinguished ourselves. It was summer time and we had mischief on our minds. We entered a small make-shift store that sold candy, American Gummy Bears for one. Since David spoke some Japanese, he would engage the proprietor at one end of the shop as a form of distraction while I loaded my pockets with those delicious Gummy Bears. True Ugly Americans!

At other times, I went out with another lad in the early evening or dusk. We each carried pellet rifles. How we got off Post with those guns still eludes me. At one end of the city nearest Camp Sendai, we shot out lamp post lighting—and got away with it. Again, Ugly Americans.

On another occasion, we took raw eggs, again at dusk, and tossed them into the thatched roof apartments that were built close to ground-level, while shouting "Banzi! Banzi!" How contemptible was that? I regret all of these Ugly American events to this very day. We walked away with impunity.

Eventually, I got my comeuppance. A friend and I had gone hiking and fishing in the countryside far from the urban area. Along the way, we hiked over field and stream and over foothills which my friend called "baby mountains." As we entered one village, we were pushing each other around a bit. Then we started sword fighting with our fishing poles. My friend kept me retreating backwards. I thought nothing of it but enjoyed thinking I was Errol Flynn, the swashbuckler. All of a sudden, I awkwardly stumbled backward and immediately knew I was literally in deep "doo doo." My "friend" had backed me into a small, uncovered "honey well." Was I an odoriferous mess? Damn right!

After climbing out amid the howling laughter of some villagers and my friend, I ran gagging to the stream that ran through the village. "Never again!" I screamed. That moment has been carved in stone in my memory bank forever and ever, as was my friend's laughing hysteria.

Upon my arrival at home, my father would not allow me to enter until I shed the soiled clothing, all except the underwear. He then put me on restriction for one week while uttering a faint sound of disgust and speaking to me with a touch of asperity. No beating or cosseting at this time, just a hot bath with soap and water. I was able to salvage my fishing pole and combat boots which I dearly loved.

My next off-base excursion was into a United States Army medical facility located outside of Sendai City. By military bus I traveled to Camp Schimmelfennig in order to have a troubling wart removed from my right ring finger. Always being a perfectionist even as a young person, the wart bothered me enough that I would peck at it until I drew blood. Not good. So off I went to the clinic. The United States military medical facilities at Sendai were spread out instead of being located at one base as is usually the case.

Upon reflection, I wonder today why the United States government named a camp after this Civil War general. It was President Lincoln who insisted on promoting Colonel Alexander Schimmelfennig to brigadier general much to the dismay and protest of Secretary of War Edwin M. Stanton. Lincoln told Stanton: "There has got to be something done…in the interest of the Dutch…and I want Schimmelfennig appointed."

Schimmelfennig historically is remembered for hiding 2-3 days in a woodshed, or outhouse, juxtaposed to an aromatic pigpen, in order to avoid capture during the Battle of Gettysburg (July, 1863). A real leader!

Most military or political generals are often remembered for military events—both positive and negative. In Schimmelfennig's case, it was strictly political correctness. But why a camp in his name in occupied Japan? I am still befogged by the notion.

Maybe Lincoln appointed Schimmelfennig to mobilize the U.S. for the war effort which might impact national strategy. After all, at the war's outset, the United States Army consisted of about 16,400 men of whom about 1,100 were commissioned officers. That is not much of an Army.

Lincoln considered the issues of slavery and emancipation that could tip the border states in the Confederacy. "I think…to lose Kentucky is …to lose the whole game. Kentucky gone, we cannot hold Missouri, nor as I think, Maryland…the job on our hands is too large for us. We would as well consent to separation at once, including the surrender of this capitol."

Lincoln never read Karl von Clauswitz's famous treatise, *On War*, but he was astute enough to have applied some of its meaningful strategy.

"The political objective is the goal, war is the means of reaching it, and means can never be considered in isolation from their purpose....war should never be thought of as something autonomous but always as an instrument of policy." (*On War*) In other words, war itself is never apart from politics as politics is always a whore's game.

Other than Camp Schimmelfenninig, I did venture to visit Japanese movie theaters showing American films with Japanese subtitles. I was most interested in the "Paramount News" clips and the vibrant voice of Gregory Abbot covering many scenes of the Korean War. Some of the black and white coverage was brutal. Even though it has been many years ago, I still recall one scene of carnage that I can never forget: A young Korean boy who had no eyes and a body no longer covered by skin but in a black crust and splotched with pus, all due to American napalm. The same scene was replicated in Vietnam. Other clips showed villages reduced to ash—again by U.S. napalm.

I always wondered why the base theater news clips were biased showing how savage the North Korean and Chinese were to Americans and South Koreans. As a young history student, I was greatly befuddled by such coverage. Today, I understand, of course. Americans never commit war crimes!

According to the late history Professor Howard Zinn, "the Korean War mobilized liberal opinion…to sustain a policy of intervention abroad, militarization of the economy and trouble for those who stayed outside the coalition…" As of today, looking at Vietnam, Iraq and Afghanistan, Professor Zinn is right on target. As a history instructor myself, it is fairly easy to conclude that the Korean War gave McCarthyism and anti-Communism a life-long transfusion of new blood.

Even Truman was caught up in the wave of Communist paranoia. In March of 1947 he issued Executive Order 9835. The purpose: To seek and find any "infiltration of disloyal persons" in the United States government. From a book by Douglas Miller and Marion Nowack, *The Fifties*, they state: "Truman…was responsible for creating…hysteria…some 1.6 million persons were investigated. Not a single case of espionage was uncovered...though 500 persons were dismissed...." This was another Red scare witch hunt conducted by the President of the United States, destroying the careers of hundreds of loyal and innocent government employees.

Then came Wisconsin Senator Joseph McCarthy who exacerbated Truman's frenzy and panic. At a Women's Republican Club in Wheeling, West Virginia (early 1950), he said: "I have here in my hand a list of 205—a list of names that were made known to the Secretary of State as being members of the Communist Party...who are working and shaping policy in the State Department."

McCarthy went on in various venues exclaiming the same distorted verbiage—not even being consistent with the same number of so-called United States government workers who were members of the Communist Party. This rhetoric went on for at least two years. Then he went even further. In 1954 he began hearings to investigate Communists in the military and movie business. He was finally censured by the United States Senate as "conduct unbecoming a member of the United States Senate." Joseph McCarthy was condemned to caricature. "Have you no decency, sir, no decency at all?"

In my history classroom, Mr. Tucker did his best to keep the atrocities of the Korean War and McCarthyism on a short leash. I felt that he didn't want to chance fogging up our patriotic zeal. We began each class with a pledge and a prayer. His students really didn't care as much as I did about history and current events. I was in a "class" all by myself, again feeling that isolation. Today, I am thankful for that interest and curiosity about history.

A marquee event occurred at Camp Sendai in 1951. A celebrity of great renown came to our school: Joe Louis, one of the greatest boxers of all time and former heavyweight champion was on tour in the Far East visiting U.S. troops. I was thrilled to have shaken his shovel-like hand, and to have spoken with him. Louis had been in a segregated Army during World War II, attaining the rank of sergeant, like Elvis.

One of the most impressive Korean veterans I ever met was named Sergeant Bright, the quintessential double for "Radar," the Company clerk in the smash TV series

"M*A*S*H." That TV series, by the way, was subliminally an allegory of Vietnam, not Korea. Sloppy uniforms, shaggy hair, undisciplined troops, including officers, were in contrast to the crew-cut prototypes of the Korean War era.

Like "Radar," Corporal Bright was a Company Clerk but on a much larger scale. He was in constant demand by the chain of command because of his shorthand, grammar and composition skills. After graduation from high school Bright attended business college prior to his draft notice in 1949. Despite enough physical handicaps to be deferred, including his eyesight and flat feet, he asked for waivers so he could serve. Elvis Presley did likewise in terms of doing his duty. He had no physical deferment, but could have negated his draft status; he chose otherwise.

Most troops in Korea did not live under the best of circumstances. But Bright was an exception. Because of his asthma, his commander secured non-wool United States Army blankets for him. All troops wore combat boots, with the exception of Bright. Because of his feet, his commander provided him with soft shoes. Bright also was afforded a private cadre room and a special mattress for his bed. More about Bright later.

Family life at Camp Sendai was engaging and very much American. Camp Jinmachi was likewise to a certain extent. My first Thanksgiving and Christmas in Japan were at Camp Jinmachi. Instead of home cooking, we as a family joined my dad's troops at the Company Mess Hall. On both holidays the place was festooned with all the trimmings and ornamentation of the season. I was enthralled with the idea of going to the Army Mess Hall wearing my combat boots. The chow was excellent. Turkey, dressing, mashed and sweet potatoes, cranberry sauce and all the rest. Best of all, we ate off compartmentalized shiny metal trays. Pumpkin pie with whipped cream followed the main courses and all the seconds and thirds one wanted. Ice cream was always on the menu. The Christmas dinner was followed by Christmas music and individual soldier singers with the traditional carols.

At Camp Sendai, the Noncommissioned Officers (NCO) Club held "Family Night" once per month. That was really enjoyable for me and the rest of the dependent children who attended. Everything was free—on the taxpayers' dime! All the Coke, Ginger Ale, ice cream and regular food one could handle, such as steak and burgers. The adults had a choice of free beer, whiskey, scotch and the like. No civvies were allowed. Soldiers had to be in uniform. The Military Police (MPs) made their rounds as well. There were very few NCOs ever escorted for being drunk or disorderly. It was truly a family night on the base.

Another aspect of family life at both camps was this: I never once saw anyone with a pet dog or pet cat. I never saw a stray dog or cat during my many excursions in the countryside, either. Did the Japanese eat their animals as do the Chinese and Koreans?

Military family life also revealed some warts. It was not all an "Ozzie and Harriet" image. There were a number of so-called "desperate housewives" who slept around, particularly after their husbands deployed to Korea, which led to a high divorce rate.

Then there was a thriving "Black Market" involving many dependent women, including my own mother. She would purchase a carton of Camel cigarettes from the Post Exchange (PX), for example, and use our houseboy as a "middle man." A single carton could be obtained for one dollar. She would then sell it to the Japanese for ten dollars, a 1000% profit minus a cut for the houseboy. The same for coffee, sugar, chocolate and most anything desired by the consumer. If apprehended, the military husband would be punished to the extent of losing rank and a fine. My mom was never caught.

More about family life at Camp Sendai, Japan. Free and cheap alcohol and tobacco are major factors in the negative health of so many military people. Every soldier, sailor, airman and marine had and has access to EM, NCO and Officer Clubs spilling over with alcohol, especially during my days growing up on military bases in the USA and overseas.

In passionate retrospect, I am angry because tobacco and alcohol for the most part touched the young lives of my dad, mom and brother, all career military. If my brother had died in Vietnam as a battle casualty (in a wrong war of American aggression), that is one thing. But to die from self-inflicted tobacco and dietary wounds is another, although being a religious extremist, he did not drink. As for my dad it was booze, tobacco and a very poor red-meat diet. My mother as well, in the final analysis. I know that "anger" and "aggression" are not healthy for "...anger resteth in the bosom of fools." (Ecclesiastes 7:9) In neuroscience parlance aggressive emotion is both hereditary and environmental. Both biological parents were trapped in chronic angry moods. Thus, my anger and aggressive issues are better understood with this knowledge.

"Family Night" often triggered unmooring flashbacks to my dad's drinking bouts. One episode in particular is still freshly etched in my mind. A short time before we departed for Japan, I recall how dad reacted to an incident that was strictly my fault. His anger and aggressive actions resulted in a mild setback to his military career.

It happened while living in Colorado Springs prior to our Rodeo Court days. Dad was stationed at Camp Carson, Colorado, so we rented a small white rambler off base. We lived in a fairly nice low middle-class environment in the southern end of the city. From the back yard across the alley and the vacant lot (full of junk cars) was a local beer joint. Very blue collar, it was. I remember walking to movies starring Gene Autry and a Three Stooges short subject. That was my favorite form of entertainment at the time. It cost 50 cents for a double feature in those days.

My dad was a regular at the beer joint on most weekends. I had an ongoing business of surreptitiously pilfering from the back of the joint used Coke and other glass pop bottles that retained a deposit. The used cases were stacked on top in vertical rows making an easy snatch. Usually at night, I would load up a number of bottles in brown paper bags; the next day I'd take them inside and collect my coins. What an entrepreneur! Clever, that is, until I was caught in the act. The owner grabbed me by the arm, took me inside and made me sit while he called my father. My dad appeared shortly thereafter. But the local cops were already in place. Was I frightened? You bet I was! My dad was already high. And he was angry—not only at me (embarrassment) but at the owner as well for calling the cops.

"Why in the (expletive deleted) didn't ya' call me instead of the police?" yelled my dad. He went on and on with the profanity. Finally, the cops told him to shut up or he'd be arrested for disturbing the peace. My dad made restitution after finding out how long I had run this shady operation. The cops departed. But dad excused himself to go the men's room. He then pulled the wall plumbing from its anchor and water was gushing all over. He continued to rip the joint up. The cops returned. They cuffed him until the Military Police arrived from Camp Carson. I was escorted home by the MPs. Dad was registered at the Post Stockade. My mother went insane, screaming at me and the MPs. Her temper raged forth in a fury. My father being from Alabama didn't like being jailed with a black soldier so he beat him bloody. Dad was then put in a separate cell.

The denouement resulted in dad being reduced in rank by one stripe and a suspended sentence attached to an Article 15 (non-judicial punishment), and loss of some pay.

One late evening a few weeks later, I was suddenly awakened from a sound sleep, sitting bolt-upright, after hearing much profanity and bellowing from my mother who was in the process of dismantling my 230 lb father with his own combat boot. She was ripping his fatigue uniform to shreds while she pummeled him. He simply gritted his teeth and did nothing. He was drunk and gobsmacked.

I'd had enough! I rumbled out of bed and rushed them both, telling them to stop. My dad never liked my aggressive ways, so he back-handed me, sending me downward to hardwood flooring, bruising my elbows. My mother repeatedly slapped him, while telling my dad never to touch me again.

That's what "Family Night" did for me, in retrospect. Very traumatic. At this time in my young life, I loved going to "Family Night" but hated the flashbacks whenever the aroma of whiskey and beer permeated my ambiance. I rarely if ever cried after being smacked by my father, partly because I was enthralled by Hercules of Greek mythology.

He is the great iconic Hellenic hero. He appears in epics, histories and tragedy and in my mind.

In myth, he was conceived by a mortal woman and fathered by Zeus. But Zeus was married to Hera who hated Zeus's sons by mortal women. Thereafter, she hated Hercules. Hercules is a hero because he endures all of Hera's attempts to kill him. Thus, his name "Hercules" means "glory through Hera" a mainstream endurance of courage.

While Hercules was a baby in his crib, Hera put two poisonous snakes next to him. Instead of crying and cowering as did his twin, Hercules grabbed and strangled the snakes with his bare hands. His image gives me spiritual strength. I always tried to emulate his non-crying living body. Hercules' exceptional strength, courage, sexual appetite, passion and worst of all, rage, seems to have infected my childhood person.

Another interesting incident of family life at Camp Sendai occurred at a local Japanese riding stable near the base. Every once in a while I patronized this stable because I love horses and horseback riding. For 300 yen (less than one dollar in 1951), I was able to ride for an hour. But one day it all fell apart. Since my dad had been in the "Mule Pack" during World War II and a blacksmith, I knew a little as to how horses should be treated and look. On this warm day, after riding with a friend, we returned the horses and walked with them into the stables which reeked. They needed mucking out; horses were thin and needed shoes, better feed and clean water.

Then the kicker: A Japanese stable boy started beating one of the horses. In a rage, I attacked him with a cudgel, smacking him in the back of his head, drawing blood and his wrath. Calmer heads prevailed. I was ostracized from that stable—but not until the military powers told them to shape up and improve conditions forthwith. That was done, according to some of my contacts. But, I never rode there again.

I did accomplish a good thing even though I caught more fury from my father. In response, I railed at him saying that I care more for animals than people and I did not feel remorse for smacking the stable boy who wanted charges against me.

So the conflict between my father and me continued well into adult life, until after high school I left home at 18 and joined the United States Army while we were stationed in Germany.

I became a court-appointed humane investigator and roamed the Commonwealth of Virginia for 20 or more years, rescuing hundreds of suffering animals, while prosecuting their perpetrators in the courts. Again, I've been reminded by the great Victorian poet, Alfred Lord Tennyson: "I have the strength of ten because my heart is pure."

Other features of family life at Camp Sendai resulted in our school arranging a field trip to a Kabuki theater performance. This event occurred in 1952, six months prior to my departure for the United States.

Kabuki theater originated in 1603 when all roles were played by men who often appear in kimonos with long sleeves and wide sashes, obviously playing the role of a female character. Kabuki themes usually deal with love and war. A narrator with background music chants the story. I was impressed with this aspect of Japanese culture since I had a secret desire to become an actor.

During the Tokugawa Period, Kabuki was suppressed because Shogunate was conservative and Kabuki was sexually oriented. Later on, Kabuki transformed into a dramatic art.

Artist Fona Rozal Brown, from Washington, DC, explores African-American culture and its influence on world cultures, especially in Japan. She has interlaced traditional Japanese Kabuki theater and African-American hip-hop, depicted in her paintings displayed at the Corcoran Gallery in Washington, DC.

Mr. Tucker exposed our eighth grade class to as much culture as possible, even though many fellow students did not like the field trips.

Regarding Japanese cuisine, Mr. Tucker spoke on occasion of "sushi," a raw fish dish wrapped in cold rice and seaweed. To me that was and still is a simple "yuk." I never tried it. No way. "Miso soup" was another menu item. This soup consisted of Ramen noodles and "sashimi," raw seafood soaked in soy sauce and horseradish, eaten with chopsticks. Again, no thank you! I remembered the oft-spoken phrase: "When bowl is miserable the brain weeps."

I was more interested in woodcrafts, lacquered black dolls, inlaid mother of pearl tables and Bunrakri theater puppet shows. By the way, Japanese invented the cultured pearl circa 1930 that led to quality pearls and a lucrative industry. The dolls fascinated me. As I recall, I carried a doll until I was nearly six years old—something to love, I assume. That doll today reminds me of poet Robert Burns' "Red, Red Rose." ("I will love thee till a the seas gang dry.")

The Shamisen guitar-like instrument also entertained me. Maybe it reminded me in some way of country music which I listened to as a child. The Koto Harp was a lovely soothing instrument to me as well. My favorite Japanese song for all time is "China Night," sung in Japanese. It has moved me to tears on many occasions.

Mr. Tucker also pointed out to my class how the Japanese adopted other aspects of Western culture, such as baseball. By the way, the Little League Aces from Japan took home the Little League World Series Title for 2010. What is more interesting is this: It ended the United States 5-year reign as title holder.

In August of 2011, the American team from California defeated the Japanese Little Leaguers 2 to 1 and regained the title. After the game, the Japanese team began sobbing uncontrollably as if they had lost the world—not a baseball game. Understandably, Japanese culture to this very day does not accept losing because it is tantamount to surrender and losing face.

Recovering from the 2011 loss, Japan's Noriatsu Osaka hit three home runs and three triples in the 2013 Little League World Series title game, defeating Tennessee's potent line-up 12-2, taking the title back to Japan.

In addition, the Japanese women's soccer team won the World Cup in 2011, defeating a very good American team. This victory will help heal the psychological wounds from the 2011 earthquake and tsunami.

Japanese Judo, Kendo (stick fighting) and Karate truly captivated my attention. The matches I saw transfixed me. Ironically, as an adult, I've studied Hapkido Karate (strictly Korean) with a fourth-degree black belt private instructor (Sensi). My exposure to Japanese Karate discernibly influenced my desire for martial arts training.

One of the most impressive features of Japanese life is not to wear shoes inside the home. To this very day, I still practice the removal of my footgear before proceeding into my abode. While entering the few Japanese homes that I was fortunate to visit, the straight rows of shoes lined at the entrances impressed me. After removing their shoes, Japanese would then step into "Getas" (a type of slipper). I remember the creaking floors that were covered to some extent with woven "tatomi mats." Their homes were sparsely decorated with furniture, with low tables here and there. Wood, straw and heavy paper made up the constructive materials, by and large. In winter, coal and kerosene provided warmth. The average Japanese struggled to keep warm in the winter. Coal and kerosene were not easily available or affordable after World War II.

The bedroom area that I remember consisted of beds of cotton quilts called "futons," while the pillow was quite small and bean-filled. Other rooms were separated by sliding panels constructed of heavy paper. As for indoor plumbing, it did not exist at this time in most average homes. Despite the austerity, this was home to these war-torn people. The small houses were clean and homey. I felt honored to have been invited into this strange but interesting world.

Mr. Tucker's history class included sessions on how the newly formed Japanese government worked (under MacArthur). Most of the students, including myself, did not understand all that he outlined for us. His main point was the 1947 Constitution which established the bicameral Diet.

Mr. Tucker emphasized the fact that the government's major objective was to prevent militarism from ever again raising its ugly head. He said the Diet was similar to the United States House of Representatives, a legislative body but also different in that a judicial branch was also a part of the Diet, unlike the United States system that has three separate branches of government. He went on to say that Japanese political districts are called "prefectures" governed by elected governors and assemblies. MacArthur's Japan was divided into cities, towns and villages.

Mr. Tucker's use of visual aids made more sense out of his civics lessons. Most of my classmates were not that interested. There were times when Mr. Tucker blew his whistle to awaken some of us who had drifted into la-la-land. One big difference that Mr. Tucker pointed out is that the Japanese had an almost 100% literacy rate, unlike much of the West, especially America. That really caught my attention and still does.

The major political party in Japan today is the Democratic Party of Japan (DPJ) under their fifth Prime Minister in the past four years. Nato Kan did not survive very long, partly because upon election he said a major consumption tax needed to be instituted in order to give Japan's flagging economy a life. Japan is suffering from the effects of deflation, and a terrible disaster, the 2011 earthquake and tsunami. Nato Kan was succeeded by Yoshiiko Noda, a Nationalist and fiscal hawk. He was Japan's seventh prime minister since 2001. Kan's government also handled badly the incident that involved a collision between a Japanese self-defense ship and a Chinese fishing boat. Kan, additionally, faced renewed territorial disputes with Russia.

In December 2012 Japanese voters returned power to the Liberal Democratic Party (LDP) that ran postwar Japan until 2009. The LDP replaced Yoshiiko Noda with Nationalist Shinzo Abe who bungled the Prime Ministership five years earlier (2006-07). He's Japan's first leader since 1949 to be given a second chance.

Abe's far right campaign speeches pledge to reverse Japan's pacifist constitution (the MacArthur Constitution), maintain his historical revisionisms about Japan's war crimes and urge Japan's rice farmers to join free-trade talks with the United States and other Pacific nations in order to reform the moribund economy.

In addition, Abe plans to thwart China's territorial ambitions in the South China Sea; also, to remind China that the Senkaku (Diaoyu) islands belong to Japan.

The South Koreans, meanwhile, are protesting Abe, promising to boycott Japanese goods. Abe was asked in Parliament if he would consider an official apology for Japanese aggression in Korea (1942). Abe's reply: "The definition of what constitutes aggression has yet to be established...." As a result, South Korea and China fulminated with invective.

Abe's stand (an inability to face historical truth), lowers my loving memory of MacArthur's Japan. Such reminds me of: "Truth is the daughter of time."

Abe will have to deal with South Korea's first female president, Park Geun-hye. She actually served as first lady at age 22 after her mother was assassinated (1974). Her father Park Chung-hee was inaugurated as South Korea's third president in 1963, later murdered in 1979.

Japan is also trying to ignore the fact that she has lost the vaunted number two world economic position to China. In a sense, Japan and China are natural trading partners because China is a developing country with a surfeit of labor, while Japan is a developed country with a shortage of labor.

According to *Bloomberg News*, concerned Japanese politicians are shifting their focus of national defense more toward China and away from Russia.

Unlike my time in MacArthur's Japan, the Japanese are facing a declining workforce, a huge national debt (like the United States), and the most rapidly graying population in the world. Japan is a society, however, that values older people—unlike the United States. Japanese politics differ today from what MacArthur intended. Present day pols are not allowed to advertise on TV or the Web, for instance. Worse, straitjacket laws regarding campaigns forbid face-to-face, populist tactics.

Values have changed from MacArthur's day. Japanese politicians maintain rowdy, ear-splitting assemblies using blaring megaphones for several hours at a time causing many people to become weary of politics, resulting, in fact, that up to 50 percent of young Japanese today do not support any political party. They say politics represent the old Japan (i.e., MacArthur's Japan). Candidates are also rude to each other on the hustings. They try to out "megaphone" each other, exacerbating the ear-slamming racket. Under these circumstances, the Prime Minister has an uphill battle trying to shepherd legislation through parliament on any given issue.

Because MacArthur believed in a free press, Japanese newspapers have progressed. The *Yomiuri Shimbun* has a wide public circulation. Japan also touts the largest number of TV and radio stations in all of Asia, another MacArthur initiative.

Mr. Tucker's classes included overviews of Japanese history as well as history of the United States. He wanted his students to know that history does not function in a vacuum but should be viewed from a broad perspective. His lectures fascinated me especially the ones dealing with Shogun warlords, the ruling class of the 16th and 17th centuries.

The Mathew Perry story caught most of our interest. He arrived in Tokyo Bay (1853) and was significant in opening the door to a 200-year closed and isolated country. Perry's "visit" eventually led to treaty rights and future commercial activity.

On my own, I continued to research Japanese history and found that the Meiji Restoration (1868-1912) planted the seeds of Japanese modernity and a centralized government. Meiji was likewise instrumental in depriving the Samurai (Warrior Class) of much of their political clout. The Tokugawa family held political power for 250 years thus giving birth to modern Japan.

I also discovered that the many Japanese civil wars were sparked by excessive taxation, a somewhat familiar theme in American history as well. (The American Revolution and The Whiskey Rebellion in the 18th century are examples).

I knew early on that reading history was one of my favorite activities. An interesting teacher like Mr. Tucker triggered an interest in his subject matter which compelled me to pursue historical study.

Mr. Tucker did not shy away from discussing religious history either. He spoke of how Buddhism and Confucianism entered Japan from Korea in the 6th century. He made us aware of the Jesuit missionary influx in Japan in the 16th century. I encountered a number of Japanese Christians in my time there.

Mr. Tucker did not hide his disdain for the militarists whom he referred to as "fanatics," like General Hideki Tojo, a cruel individual who set the standard for torture, beheadings and the rape of "comfort women" (Japanese Army sex slaves, mostly Korean and Chinese women). During the Rape of Nanking (World War II), many Japanese soldiers raped women and after completing the sex act, chopped their heads off.

Lt John S. Wilpers was the Army officer who arrested Prime Minister Hideki Tojo (1945) after he attempted suicide by shooting himself. MacArthur's orders were simple: find Tojo and bring him back alive. Tojo was tried and hanged as a war criminal during the Tokyo War Crimes Trial (1948).

Conservative Japanese politicians today refuse to acknowledge these monstrous war crimes—a glaring example of right-wing revisionism preventing closure for the victims.

Japan's Supreme Court in 2007 upheld a ruling denying compensation to petitioning Chinese women forced to provide sex for Japanese troops. Similar rulings affected a number of Chinese and other Asians forced into slave labor in Japanese mines and construction companies.

Something interesting: After the surrender in 1945, Japan set up a system of licensed brothels to service American soldiers. Thousands of women were employed. In the spring of 1946, General MacArthur shut them down. He felt that the "comfort issue" created an atmosphere of coercion. This was a sensitive time and MacArthur believed in women's rights, much to the disappointment of most American G.I.s.

As a youngster at this time, I was cognizant of Japanese prostitutes as I mentioned earlier. Licensed and controlled brothels made a lot of sense to me then—and now. There is a precedent for U.S. government-sponsored strumpets. During the Civil War, Union soldiers were allowed to visit prostitutes in the city of New Orleans, then under the command and control of Union troops led by General Butler who shaped the war by treating escaped slaves as contraband not to be returned to the South.

These ladies of ill-repute did not like General Butler and his ilk. On many occasions, these Southern belles in the morning would wait until the officers started walking down the street near the cathouse. Moving to the edge of the balcony, these "refined" women would then dump their chamber pots on top of these Union soldiers.

General Butler then ordered them to stop or they would be treated as enemy combatants. In response, those Southern chamber pot makers included a full color photo of General Butler on the very bottom of said pots!

I knew of several G.I.s from my father's unit who cavorted with trollops, some of them contacting a sexually transmitted disease. Controlled prostitution prevents such calamities. The "Bunny Ranch" in Nevada is a prime example of selling regulated sex—a service needed in any society. As stated previously, the Union Army provided bordellos for their troops. A smart move! As Jesus said: "Man does not live by bread alone." Thank goodness for people like Hugh Hefner and his *Playboy* bunnies.

My attention turns back to the Korean War. In June 1951 after the massive Chinese attempt to re-capture Seoul, Chinese officials agreed to discuss a possible cease fire, armistice and a mutual withdrawal of troops from the 38th Parallel.

Nineteen fifty-two was a year of endless and non-productive talks. Dwight Eisenhower's profound speech on October 24, 1952, said: "…a small country, Korea, has been for more than two years, the battleground…I am going to state the unvarnished truth…the Korean War was never inevitable…the Secretary of State (Dean Acheson) announced…that the nations outside this {defense} perimeter no person can guarantee…against military attack… On that day…diplomatic failure of this administration…sealed the…{fate of Korea}… I shall go to Korea…."

I read the *Stars and Stripes* version of his speech that had been extracted from the October 24, 1952, edition, p. 8. Ike's speech impressed me. He would make a good president, so I thought at that time. Little did I know then that he had organized his own death camps (over 200) in Germany (circa 1945), as mentioned earlier.

In January 1952, my family was set to return to the United States, my dad's tour of duty nearly complete. My mother's health greatly improved and once again my school year was interrupted. I was not happy about this turn of events. Not at all.

Sergeant Bright ("Radar") was also about to complete his tour. Upon his return from Korea, Sergeant Bright landed in my dad's unit at Camp Sendai. He was an after-dinner guest at our military quarters in Camp Sendai. Bright was a skilled raconteur. His Korean war stories dazzled me. Bright said there was little comfort for soldiers suffering from combat stress, other than the chaplain's office. Sergeant Bright, who later became an administrative aide to the battalion commander, was actually like the Remington Rear Echelon Mother Fuckers (REMF) of the Vietnam era, as he never saw combat but he did encounter many soldiers with psychological injuries, similar to "post-traumatic stress syndrome" which has affected thousands of American G.I.s in Iraq and Afghanistan.

I could feel his pain when he spoke. I never forgot his fixed glazed eyes as he told of the terror that his buddies encountered in Korea, namely "collateral damage" (the killing of helpless civilians), and the insidious use of napalm, a jellied gasoline that burned flesh to the bone. Bright said when he took short day passes, he saw homeless children struggling to survive. They were hungry, dirty and dressed in rags. While speaking, tears welled up in his eyes. He touched me deeply.

Sergeant Bright was special. He did not have to accept his draft notice, let alone go to Korea. His vision made him "4-F"—unfit for military service. Because he was a patriot he was able to obtain a waiver. After basic training which nearly killed him, he was assigned to administrative duties within the command structure.

He was beloved by his unit commander. Sergeant Bright had highly honed secretarial skills, such as shorthand and he could make a typewriter sing.

The general staff knew they had a pearl in Bright at that time in terms of his skills. Officers can always have a stronger command structure when they know their paperwork is efficiently produced. Corporal Bright eventually became Sergeant Bright because of his self-promotion to Sergeant via the Commander's approving signature.

Bright was also aware of what the historians call "fragging" which is primarily a reference to the Vietnam War. He handled papers regarding such happenings of stressed- out low-ranking soldiers' attempts on their leaders' lives. I had never heard of such a thing. Sergeant Bright knew I had an interest in Greek mythology, especially about Hercules and Ajax, Greek warriors. He said during one of Ajax's dark moments of combat stress, he ventured to murder his commanding officer; instead, he entered into a dissociate mental imbalance or simple rage and took his wrath out on helpless animals. Upon re-entry into the real world, Ajax realized what he had done and literally fell upon his own sword.

Sergeant Bright's point was that combat fatigue was nothing new to the Korean War. I sat enraptured. American POWs in Korea witnessed the so-called intense "brain washing" that affected many causing defection to the North.

As an adult historian, when relating this account to my classes, I often asked them if such psychological wounds ever heal. What does war do to the human mind? Is it thinkable to restore the wounded's humanity? With the huge number of Army suicides among Iraq and Afghanistan war veterans, it doesn't seem possible in many cases. War has an insatiable appetite for destruction.

One wonders, then, if Iraq and Afghanistan (like Vietnam) is worth the cost of blood and treasure. Also wondering why the pols do not heed George Santyana's caveat: "He who does not know history is fated to repeat it."

Because of Western technology, Mr. Tucker made the case for Japan's survival and growth. He started with Commodore Mathew Perry and his Yankee warships as they entered Tokyo Bay shattering Japan's isolationism (1853-54), while flying American flags showing 31 stars.

The same body of water also accommodated the Battleship Missouri as General MacArthur accepted the unconditional surrender document from the Imperial Japanese. In fact, the Missouri was in proximity of Perry's ship – also flying the flag of 31 stars, along with the "Stars and Stripes."

Prior to departing Camp Sendai in 1952, one of my final history classes dealt with Mr. Tucker's lecture about a great Japanese teacher (Sensi) named Yoshida (circa 1854).

He presented Yoshida as a Great Man of history. As a teacher myself, I always raised the question: "Do the men make the times or do the times make the man?" Since I've always believed in the Great Man Theory of History, the answer to the query is: The times have to be right for the Great Man. Yoshida fits.

Yoshida was a visionary. He said Japan's ban on foreign travel was like "a person in a dark room holding his breath." In 1854 it was a crime to attempt to leave Japan—a decree of Shogun who kept Japan in a "dark room" for over 200 years.

Yoshida wanted to go West with Perry, feeling that Japanese scholars needed to travel and study abroad. Shogun law put Yoshida to death at age 29 for such a revolutionary thought. Yoshida's final statement: "If my companions…take over my task, the seed of the future will not die."

Yoshida was a Samurai with an open mind. He was skilled in martial arts, a voracious reader and like the Greeks believed in a sound mind and sound body concept. Mr. Tucker added his own touch to the conclusion of Yoshida's story: "When you stop learning you stop living." He said Yoshida was a skilled swordsman, scholar and educator. In fact, Yoshida, while in Hagi Prison, taught fellow inmates hoping to restore their pride or hubris. Today, there is a wax figure of Yoshida in the Hagi Museum. Mr. Tucker said Yoshida was a founding father in the making of modern Japan.

In mid-January (1952) my brother, sister, father and mother traveled an overnight train to Yokohama. As before, our hold baggage preceded our departure. By this time, my mother had regained most of her strength, strong enough to sail on to the USA. Brother and baby sister were excited. My dad was being reassigned to Colorado Springs in the area of cryptology. I hated to leave; most of all, I didn't want to disrupt my school year. The Military Sea Transportation Service (MSTS) always provided military families with more than adequate living quarters and dining arrangements. That was a positive.

As before, I anticipated a few stormy days with the seesaw rocking of the vessel, high waves and some sleepless nights. Best of all, there would be another party while crossing the International Date Line. At the Yokohoma staging area, I witnessed some interesting observations: Black soldiers married to Japanese war brides. Some already had mixed-race babies. I felt sorry for the children as they would have a hard time assimilating in a predominately white society back home. Remember, this was not long after President Truman had integrated the Armed Services (1947). I do not recall ever seeing black students in any of my classes at Camp Jimanchi or Camp Sendai.

Dining on MSTS vessels was always something to look forward to. One old menu appeared in my scrap book which brought me back to my voyage in 1952. A brief overview of that day's fare:

> Various baby foods
> Shrimp cocktail
> Chilled celery, Indian relish, Pickles, Stuffed olives
> Minestrone a la Milanese or Cup Beef Bullion
> Cold dish: Ham – American cheese – Liverwurst – Potato salad
> Baked fresh halibut stead
> Roast prime ribs of beef au jus

Yorkshire pudding
Broccoli vinaigrette
Carrots and peas
Baked Idaho potatoes
Dutch apple pie   Fresh fruit   Strawberry Melba
Assorted nuts   Rye bread
Coffee Tea   Cocoa   Milk Tropical cold drink

There was also a calorie count on this menu. Very impressive for the 1950s, especially for the military.

The thought of leaving Japan sent me into a moment of winsome, head-snapping emotional angst, reminding me in retrospect of my favorite opera, Puccini's *Madam Butterfly*, set in Nagasaki, Japan, in 1904.

The emotional tilt in *Butterfly* best describes my emotional state at this time. Beautiful Butterfly (Cio-Cio-San) is located in a resplendent and effulgent setting with flower gardens, pine branches and flowering cherry trees, birds singing—all outside Pinkerton's rented house. This scene always reminds me of my childhood Shangri-La. The house was put together with match-box-like walls, paper-made sliding panels, all situated on top of a hill reminding me so much of Ski Hill at Camp Jinmachi.

In another scene, Butterfly appears in the flower garden awaiting an arranged marriage with Pinkerton, a blond, blue-eyed handsome naval officer. Pinkerton was pompous and hubristic. He was in port on R&R for a short stay, like most sailors, looking for an arousing sexual encounter.

Butterfly's lovely surroundings, complete with duck pond, pet rabbits and singing birds, took me back to my memory of Camp Jinmachi. Butterfly's servants reminded me of our houseboy at Camp Jinmachi who was likewise sincere, efficient and loyal.

Butterfly was deeply in love with Pinkerton. But Pinkerton took the marriage akin to monkeyshine. After all, a sailor on port call is in need of sexual relief. That is the human condition—willy-nilly. Butterfly renounces her faith and embraces Christianity to satisfy Pinkerton while disappointing her relatives. Such reminds me of our young houseboy taking up with Christianity during his employment with us.

The musical score for *Butterfly* exemplifies that of passion and romance. Opera is a marriage of words and music. Pinkerton departs for a three-year hiatus. Butterfly is sad but confident he will return. I always believed that one day, I, too, should reappear in Japan.

Three years pass. One chrome-bright day, Pinkerton's ship is spotted in the distance. Butterfly orders her maid to fill the house with flowers. She then applies make-up and dresses in her wedding gown. She is thrilled!

I experienced similar elations upon my mother's semi-recovery from her illness and my father's never going to Korea. At twilight, Butterfly and her maid, along with her blond, blue-eyed child, look for Pinkerton through small peepholes in the paper window panels. Pinkerton approaches the house. A disconcerted Butterfly tears up. She notices a strange blond woman at his side. Butterfly asks Sharpless (the American Consul) about this female. Sharpless tells her it is Pinkerton's American wife. The cruel truth dawns upon Butterfly. "All is dead for me," she cries. She slowly draws a dagger from inside her sleeve. The inscription on the blade reads: "Die with honor if it is impossible to live with honor."

Butterfly opens the creaking, sliding door, sees her child, blindfolds him, gives him a doll and an American flag, then plunges the razor-sharp dagger into her stomach; the dagger tumbles to the floor.

Pinkerton cries out: "Butterfly! Butterfly!" as he kneels beside her, sobbing with grief and shame. I identified with her stygian, inconsolable grief as I prepared to depart my Shangri-La.

The *Heat of the Sun* by David Rain is a recently published novel about Butterfly's son, Ben Pinkerton II, or "Trouble" as he was known in Nagasaki. "Trouble" thinks Kate Pinkerton is his real mother, but has doubts about his shadowy past. Ben hates his father but doesn't know why. There are a number of twists and a hint of American imperialism in this story. It is never dull but not believable, according to the reviews.

At the time, I looked for strength in MacArthur's mantra about "duty, honor and country," his ringing words on the grass-covered plain at West Point. "Faith, hope, and character build courage," he said. "They make you strong when you are weak. They teach you to be humble in success. They teach you sacrifice in the face of danger and even death." MacArthur's words stuck with me throughout my formative years. I joined the United States Army upon graduation from high school, inspired by Generals MacArthur and Ridgeway.

MacArthur himself was motivated by his readings of the *Meditations of Marcus Aurelius* who said: "A man must stand erect, not be kept erect by others." MacArthur refers to the American soldier as standing proud and tall on his own stead. I too had to stand tall at this depressing moment in my life.

Aurelius states further that "men exist for the sake of one another." MacArthur speaks of the American man-at-arms as reliable, brave, noble and strong in character, never forgetting how to weep and not to take oneself too seriously. Above all, MacArthur spoke of the long, gray line; those who never fail one another in peace or war, who exist for one another.

Marcus Aurelius also said: "Judge every word and deed… and not be diverted by the blame which follows from any people." This quote goes to the point that MacArthur was always his own man. The blame for crossing the 38th Parallel is not MacArthur's alone, but those in government who urged him to do so.

As a soldier, MacArthur during World War II went on his "Island Hopping Campaign" to weaken the Imperial Army; he drove the North Koreans back across the 38th Parallel, and he was ready to deal with Red China and Mao Tse Tung, which might have melted the Asian branch of the Cold War and would have sent Stalin a serious message.

MacArthur was carried away by the events of the times, by a violent stream of political correctness and simple green-eyed, grudging envy. On the other hand, some saw MacArthur in revolt against his own government. An op-ed piece dated December 5, 1993, in *The Washington Post*, implies that MacArthur may have been responsible for the events on December 8, 1941, at Clark Field, when half of the United States long-range bomber fleet was destroyed on the ground by Japanese planes 10 hours after the Pearl Harbor alert.

The article suggests that MacArthur wanted to thwart the use of long-range bombers against the Japanese homeland because of The General's love of the Philippines and not wanting to pull the Philippines into the Pacific war. MacArthur's troop critics wrote a dark parody of *"The Battle Hymn of the Republic"* which read in part:

> "Mine eyes have seen MacArthur
> With a bible on his knee,
> He is pounding out
> Communiqués for guys
> Like you and me,…
> And while possibly a rumor
> Now, someday 'twill be a
> Fact. That the Lord
> Will hear a deep voice say,
> Move over, God, it's Mac."

It was Shakespeare who said: "Some men are born great, some achieve greatness, and some have greatness thrust upon 'em." In Douglas MacArthur's case, all three categories befit The General.

Contributing retrospective from John Dower's book *Embracing Defeat*.

MacArthur was the Supreme Commander for the Allied Powers (SCAP). The General was instrumental in dressing Emperor Hirohito (1901-1989) in new clothes. He was the grandson of the Meiji Emperor (1868-1912). Hirohito's grandfather took the "Charter Oak Oath" at age 14. Hirohito became Emperor of Japan in 1926 at age 25. He gave "Imperial Sanction" to Japanese war crimes.

MacArthur sent the Emperor on "hat-tipping tours," speaking to the hoi polloi, causing him to evolve from God to Mortal to Symbol, "to come down from the clouds." People gawked and wept upon seeing him.

Many, however, like the poet Miyoshi Tatsuji, wanted the Emperor to abdicate and take responsibility for the war. They wanted him to accept the Buddhist concept of repentance, to retire and become a symbol of poverty, emptiness, and turn over the imperial resources to the people.

But a MacArthur aide (General Fuller) acted as a *deus ex machina* and advised The General not to allow an abdication. Without a titular head, Japan would be plunged into chaos and mayhem. MacArthur told Washington that if the Emperor were tried as a war criminal, he would need a million more troops to quell the riots.

Chief prosecutor Joseph Keenan (Tokyo War Crimes) said Hirohito was off limits. Others feared that the Emperor might commit Seppuku or be assassinated by a left-wing Communist.

The humanized Emperor was socially inept (like MacArthur), short, slight, round-shouldered, in poor physical condition, having a weak chin, high-pitched voice, face full of moles (in Japan this was considered good luck), a stubbly mustache, a straggly beard, needing a shave, thick horn-rimmed glasses, poor eye-sight, was awkward, unkempt and wore scruffy shoes (needing an 82nd Airborne spit-shine).

Upon visiting a black market in Yokohama, he said: "Interesting." On Hiroshima: "There seems to be considerable damage there."

The Emperor was also known as the "Ah-so" Emperor which means: "Oh, is that so?" He only toured clean, swept-up places which led left-wing cartoonists to call him "the Broom."

Many Japanese bottled his bath water. Others said he could swim in the rain while holding an umbrella. Some said he could put a fan between his toes and fan himself. Then there were those who collected pebbles where he walked. Thankfully, the tours ended in 1948, prior to my arrival in Japan.

It was MacArthur's occupation that called for self-criticism, apology and most of all: **RETRIBUTION.**

The Old Man (The General) was the blue-eyed Tokugawa Shogun, the belly-button of Japan, Heaven's message to Japan, the Kabuki hero who ended Japanese feudalism, was the military dictator who lived a proconsul's remoteness (like Hirohito), "who lived above the clouds" and gave Japan a constitution which was a hollow patina of the Meiji Constitution (which emphasized Duties) while the MacArthur Constitution promoted Rights.

The General, like the Emperor, never toured Japan to see things for himself or speak to the commons. His daily routine rarely changed: He arrived early each day and departed at 4 p.m. with military fanfare.

He took up residence across from the Emperor's house. It is said that if one were to arise early, one could see the Supreme Commander through the morning mist walking on the water of the palace moat.

Sayonara
"Goodbye, Tired World! I'm Going Home. Thou Art Not My Friend and I'm Not Thine." – Ralph Waldo Emerson

VIII

Fyodor Dostoevsky wrote: "Nothing is easier than denouncing the evildoer; nothing more difficult than understanding him."

The motivation for relating my story came about in a complex maze. For openers, on June 7, 2007, I was inspired while attending a Smithsonian Associates seminar: "Japan and America—Partners Facing a Changing World," featuring guest speakers: His Excellency Ryozo Kato, Japan's Ambassador to the United States; the Honorable Howard H. Baker, Jr., former Ambassador to Japan; Michael Green, holder of the Japan Chair at the Center for Strategic and International Studies; and former career diplomat Walter L. Cutler who served as host and moderator.

As a member of a large C-Span audience, I was electrified by the many salient issues discussed. Upon completion of the give-and-take, the Q and A session followed. Seated close to the stage, I raised my hand and addressed my question to Ambassador Kato concerning Japan's slaughter of whales, dolphins and sharks (fins for soup). I mentioned that Japan alone took over 10,000 whales in 2007 in violation of the ban on commercial whaling.

Ambassador Kato's reply was simple: "We took them for 'scientific research'." At that point, former Senator Howard Baker spoke up and in effect said that the Ambassador's response was so much blather and poppycock.

I was elated to finally hear a politician speak the truth. At that moment, the light blinked. I knew then that I had to tell the story of my life in Japan, from an historical and childhood experience.

During his tour of duty in Japan, Senator Baker said he saw a liberal quantity of whale meat for sale at the food markets and that it tasted like rubber. Fried dolphin is also available at these fish stands, according to Greenpeace.

The dolphin bloodbath takes place near the small village of Taiji on southern Honshu where 2000 dolphins are lured into a "cove" and bludgeoned to death in a bloody ritual, reminding me of the brutal treatment of Americans on the Bataan Death March.

The Japanese who eat dolphin are ignorant of the mercury content and ignore the cruelty to animals, a reminder again of the beheadings during World War II in terms of a total Japanese disregard for human and animal suffering.

Yet, another motivating factor: A recent World Society for the Protection of Animals (WSPA) report says that over two million dogs are caged, tortured and slaughtered every year by the dog meat industry in both Koreas. My wrath flashed when reading the data: Are Asians in general immune to animal suffering?

The report further states that breeder dogs are bred until their reed-thin, frail bodies die. Korean restaurants offer popular Korean dishes including "stewed dog leg" and "spicy deep-fried dog," according to *The Washington Post* (Nov 27, 2010, A6).

Why, then, does the United States government defend a country which systematically engages in animal suffering (namely dogs) when Eagle quarterback Michael Vick served two years in prison for dog-fighting cruelties? The answer, of course: political expediency. Once again, the hypocrisy of U.S. foreign policy.

I was also inspired by Bob Hunter, the founder of Greenpeace in 1975 when his team thwarted a Soviet whaling vessel from killing whales. Bob's team lowered inflatable rafts and positioned themselves between the Soviet ship and the whales.

A harpoon fired over Hunter's head nearly killed him. The Soviets soon departed *sans* dead whales.

The International Whaling Commission in 1986 placed a moratorium on commercial whaling. Since then, the Japanese have taken over 20,000 whales according to Greenpeace. Once again, Japan does not worry about international law.

Japan is not alone culpable in killing whales. Iceland and Norway do their share of murder as well. But they do not take dolphins or sharks. Norwegian Animal Rights organizations have marshaled over 1,000 signatures to end the whale massacre, according to the WSPA.

Greenpeace and the brave crew of the *Sea Shepherd* have foiled many Japanese whalers' attempts to slaughter more whales. The Japanese whaler *Nisshin Maru* and Greenpeace's *Sea Shepherd* are known for their confrontations. In 2008, for example, the *Sea Shepherd* obstructed a refueling attempt of the *Nisshin Maru*.

In 2010 the *Sea Shepherd*'s dropped boat's bow was sheared off after the whaler *Shonan Maru* deliberately rammed the boat that was harassing the Japanese fishing fleet on a whale hunt. Whale meat is officially sanctioned by the Japanese government disguised as "salted stuff" while it is shipped to various locations.

As a candidate, President Obama promised to end illegal whaling. His words have fallen upon deaf ears and they ring hollow.

Greenpeace has also been active in monitoring radiation levels, taking soil and crop samples and speaking with earthquake and tsunami survivors. Greenpeace says that nuclear radiation surrounding the Fukushima site will last forever. More than 140,000 people, according to Greenpeace, have been permanently evacuated from the farms and villages in and around Fukushima.

The possible extinction of Bluefin tuna is another deplorable violation by Japanese fisherman. Bluefin tuna is a mainstay of sushi, a favorite in most Japanese eateries and homes. According to *The Washington Post* (March, 2010, p. 11) Bluefin tuna stock has declined 74 percent the past 50 years.

Bluefin tuna is displayed in Tokyo's Tsukiji Fish Market. When I visited Tokyo in 1950, I never saw anything so grotesque. A single Bluefin tuna today sells for thousands of dollars at the market, according to *The Washington Post* (March, 2010, p.11). Tuna are remarkable: they can weigh up to 1,500 pounds and swim as fast as 43 miles per hour.

Early morning people watch the auction at the Tsukiji Fish Market, looking at the vast amount of seafood, some still flapping. Many eat sushi for breakfast.

As a child in Japan, the Buddhist reverence for all life dominated my thinking about animal suffering. Today, the fact that 150,000 dolphins die each year in tuna nets operated by Japanese and Mexican fishing boats affect me now as much as it did then.

Another motivating factor inspiring this narrative is the ethereal cherry-blossom season in Washington, D.C., beginning each April. Since my days in Washington, D.C. (1959-Present), I am always reminded of my Shangri-La upon visiting the cherry blossoms.

They came to Washington in 1912. It was first lady Helen Taft and Eliza Sudmore who planted the initial cherry tree. Sudmore was partially responsible for bringing the trees to Washington, D.C. Japanese Viscountess Iwa Chinda planted the second tree. She was the wife of Ambassador Chinda.

Japanese plants aside from the cherry trees have become an integral part of most American landscapes, including the Tidal Basin and the White House with beautiful Japanese Maples; fall Chrysanthemums are displayed at the U.S. Capitol and the Library of Congress. Star Magnolias are also on view at the Library and offer a bright flowering in March.

In a word, American gardens *without* Japanese plants would not be recognizable. Most Azaleas and Lilies also came from Japan. The Ginko tree which I thought was Chinese actually came from Japan.

To help me "understand" more about the Japanese, I read the thoughts and emotions of a young Japanese Kamikaze pilot and *The New York Times* best seller, *The Flyboys* by James Bradley.

Yasuo Kuwahara's story as told to American historian Gordon T. Allred (in 1951) is powerful. I attended Bradley's book signing in Washington, D.C., and spoke with him briefly about my stay in Japan.

These accounts gave me reason to better "understand" Japan, the evildoer, in all aspects of its World War II atrocities and whaling violations.

It was Yasuo's opening comments that speak volumes in terms of why wars occur: collective ignorance. Yasuo's memoirs' underlying theme is driven by the notion of divine heritage and the "Spirit of Bushido." He is asked at the beginning of his Kamikaze training: "Are you willing to give your life as a divine son of the great Nippon empire and Emperor?"

His Kamikaze training started as early as high school, and then was transferred to Hiro Air Base in Western Honshu with the Fourth Fighter Squadron. He studied aeronautics and glider flying in his early course studies. But he went through literal torment during his basic training as did all other future pilots. His instructors perpetrated crimes upon their bodies. Yasuo describes Yoshiro Tsubaki, his dull instructor: "A small man with a supple, whip-like body, a hatchet face and reptilian eyes."

Similar to Kamikaze training, one must note Japan's national sport: Sumo wrestling which has a 1500 year history. It is known as the sport of emperors. The young wrestler, like the young Kamikaze pilot, is mauled with metal baseball bats in addition to beer bottle beatings and cigarette burnings in an attempt to make him tough and disciplined. Sumo training (like World War II Kamikaze shaping) is largely self-governed.

In 2008, a young student wrestler named Takashi Saito decided to leave his Sumo stable. Similar to a Kamikaze pilot trying to leave, the results are fatal. Raging instructors with "hatchet faces" and "reptilian eyes" are known to beat their young students to death. The Japanese Sumo Association (JSA) is currently investigating Saito's death.

Kamikaze pilots were taught that "honor was heavier than mountains and death lighter than a feather." Over 5,000 young men covenanted with death. Not all were fanatics. Yasuo Kuwahura was in comparison a gentle soul. Some were not above weeping for their mothers. MacArthur said this about American soldiers as well.

As Allred said: "Yasuo was one of those at fifteen hurled into one of the most terrifying holocausts of history." Yasuo even survived the atomic blast on Hiroshima on August 6, 1945, at 8:15:17.

Since 1945, the American way of life necessitates a global military dominance along with the use of aggressive military power, e.g., the atomic bomb, Star Wars weapons, napalm and the like.

According to Andrew J. Bacevich's and John W. Dower's latest tomes: *America's Path To Permanent War,* and Dower's *Culture of War: Pearl Harbor/Hiroshima/9-11/Iraq* says: "Osama bin Laden and Harry Truman justified wanton killing with essentially the same Manichean rhetoric…the ability to separate good from evil make killing easy." Such notions have pushed the United States into a state of perpetual war with enemies everywhere. Therefore, in the name of "security," Vietnam, Iraq and Afghanistan justifies the American war machine to roll on and spend billions. This treasure could be used to reshape cities like Detroit, rebuild infrastructure, schools, revamp the health care system, and above all, control environmental destruction and reduce the avarice in American society.

Otherwise, America is on the road to Perdition, the Devil's house, the everlasting lake of fire, the abode of the damned and the home of lost souls. In 1963, during a maniacal cabinet meeting regarding Vietnam, Attorney General Robert Kennedy asked the question: "Why not withdraw?" According to Arthur Schlesinger, who was present said: "The question hovered…then died away." This sums up the stupefaction of United States foreign policy.

There was an incident on Saipan near the end of the war when a pilot actually carried out a Kamikaze mission on his own airport hangers, destroying several Japanese airplanes because he wanted to see an end to the war. He was a fanatic for the right reason.

After engaging Bradley's *Flyboys*, I ended with mixed emotions. Bradley states that the Emperor system allowed for militarism, imperialism, biological experiments by Unit 731, cannibalism of American pilots' livers and thigh flesh (taken while many were alive), added to sukiyaki stew dinners, and millions of beheadings (actually more prisoners of all stripes died from beheadings than those fried in the Hiroshima bombing).

Bradley used a terror balance sheet to mention American war atrocities stemming from the 1864 Colorado Sand Creek Massacre when about 600 Cheyenne Indian women and children were massacred by United States Army troops led by the Reverend John Chivington and the governor of Colorado. These Indians were under the protection of President Lincoln. United States soldiers severed male organs and female vaginas—wearing the female private part on their hats. Illiterate western icon and Indian hunter, Kit Carson, called Chivington a "dog."

The author then describes General Curtis LeMay's order to firebomb (with napalm) Tokyo (1945) killing over 100,000 civilians. Bradley writes: "Peoples' heads exploded in the heat, liquid brains…burst in their skulls bubbling an eerie fluorescent."

Bradley also says President T. Roosevelt caused the deaths of over 250,000 Filipinos during the Philippine insurrection, most of them non-combatants. T.R's policy was to take no POWs.

"Understanding" at this juncture was again troubling at best. I was unable to process the balance sheet of terror.

I kept thinking of my Shangri-La—how could all of this horror be real?

Many eyewitness atrocities were documented by the late Herbert L. Zincke who kept a secret diary called "Mitsui Madhouse," published in 2003.

Zincke was held as a POW in Japan for 40 months after his capture in 1941 while he was stationed at Clark Air Force Base in the Philippines. While captive, he saw vile crimes perpetuated against all forms of life by Japanese soldiers which flies in the face of Japanese Buddhism's deep devotion for such existence.

Zincke and other U.S. prisoners were roped together and forced to march for miles in blistering hot sun without water. Many collapsed from exhaustion. These shriveled humans were then shot or ruthlessly beheaded.

On one such march, a horse buckled from simple fatigue. Zincke records that he saw Japanese soldiers gather around the helpless and convulsing animal, each taking a turn bayoneting the horse until it died. The guards then had the cooks grind the meat into burgers.

Zincke spent many of his days shoveling coal, stacking lumber and carrying 120 pound bags of rocks; he only weighed 122 pounds himself! When he became too weak to arise from bed, he was then beaten by Japanese guards with stone-like bamboo clubs.

Zincke developed beriberi because of a lack of thiamine in his meager diet causing his legs to swell like balloons from the knees down.

On his worst days, he felt suicidal, depressed and hating his captors. But after hearing of General LeMay's firebombing of Tokyo, Zincke's outrage re-energized his will to live.

Fellow POWs were often tortured beyond human imagination. Some had their fingernails pulled out—slowly! Others had bamboo slivers shoved under their nails. The slivers were then ignited and allowed to burn.

Then there were those prisoners who were hanged upside down. All of a sudden, a flood of urine and iodine came rushing into their nostrils, a perverse version of urine and iodine-boarding. One wonders why the CIA didn't think of this form of torture during the Iraq war.

What mystery! What mayhem! What suffering! In 2011, the mayhem and suffering returned to Japan set in opposition to their ancient state of refinement and magic. The conqueror is most always conquered!

Zincke's release came in September 1945.

The central theme of Bradley's book is overshadowed by this so-called balance sheet of terror. Bradley's main thrust is the story of eight Flyboys who crashed on Chichi Jima about 150 miles from Iwo Jima. The ninth pilot was George H. W. Bush who was rescued by a United States submarine. The other Flyboys were POWs on Chichi Jima, a very important communication link between the Pacific and Imperial Headquarters in Tokyo. The Flyboys were sent to bomb Chichi Jima.

While the flag was being raised on Iwo Jima for the second time, the eight Flyboys were beheaded the same day on Chichi Jima. The United States government covered up this atrocity for all these years because they did not want the Flyboys' parents to know how they died. Similarly, I suspect the same cover-up regarding the death of Ranger Pat

Tillman, who sacrificed his lucrative NFL career to fight Taliban in Afghanistan. The true cause of his death was negated by the United States Army at the time.

Bradley points out that MacArthur allowed one of Japan's most notorious war criminals to go free. Colonel Masanobu Tsuji had preserved Chinese heads in his office. He personally beheaded Flyboys. Bradley states that... "Colonel Tsuji was not prosecuted on orders from MacArthur because of political expediency. He had anti-communist bona fides...and had acute planning skills needed for the post-war occupation. Colonel Tsuji was eventually elected to Japan's lower house in the Japanese Diet."

This miscarriage of justice reminds me of another criminal: the former Nazi and S.S. Major W. von Braun who became a United States citizen because he was a rocket scientist and eventually a NASA celebrity.

I am also disturbed by the modern day pilgrimage of Japanese politicians to the Yasukuni Shrine which honors Japan's war dead, including General Tojo and other war criminals.

Yet not one American has ever been tried for a war crime, according to Bradley. Then again, winning or losing largely determines war crimes. It was Cicero who said: "During war, all laws are silent."

Speaking of American war crimes and crimes against humanity there is a paper trail for sure, according to *Time* magazine (Oct 18, 2010, p. 30). Note the following:

1906 - Harvard doctor infects Filipino convicts with cholera to study the effects. Survivors were compensated with cigars.

1930's – Tuskegee study halted care for black men infected with syphilis so doctors could study the disease.

1946-1948 – U.S. doctors infected 700 Guatemalans with syphilis to test penicillin.

1951 – The CIA allegedly spreads LSD over a French town where witnesses had a sudden outbreak of hallucinations.

1950s – U.S. doctors injected unwitting patients with plutonium and the "Atomic soldiers" were exposed to radiation after testing atomic bombs in the Nevada desert.

The U.S. Army prosecuted Nazi and Japanese war criminals in 1945 for waterboarding (Bush/Cheney) and for similar chemical experiments on live human beings. Now, James Bradley's terror balance sheet makes sense to me.

This childhood adventure has helped me to "understand" my Existentialist reason for being. My sense of spiritual renewal, an uplift, some degree of redemption regarding my torments, hoping I've avoided what Freud called "mendacity" (with reference to memoir-like tales), looking square at my "soul eye," leaving my personal journey of anguish behind and becoming a witness to real life while re-experiencing the events that I've known to be true, best to my recollection.

Psychologists know that people tend to become more "understanding" and forgiving as they grow older. The first ever United States delegation witnessed a Japanese ceremony commemorating history's first use of an atomic bomb 68 years ago. Then President George H. W. Bush attended the funeral of Hirohito in 1989. Bush went to Hawaii on December 7, 1991, where he stood before Japanese and American veterans of World War II and said: "I hold no rancor in my heart for my former enemy." Enough said. Dostoevsky's words are enshrined forevermore.

A cloud-covered slate-gray day with lowering skies hovered over the Brobdingnagian troop ship on the bloodshot sunrise of a tortured departure from my beloved Shangri-La. Screeching tugboats struggled to move our ship out of Yokohama Harbor as the snow-tipped beauty of Mt. Fuji faded from my view. I was gripped by a sense of melancholy, feeling on the blue side of lonesome and looking for Heartbreak Hotel while saying "Sayonara." The lyrics of one of Eddy Arnold's greatest country hits of the 1960's captured my gloomy feelings of joylessness at this time:

> *"Make the world go away*
> *And get it off my shoulder*
> *Say the things you used to say*
> *And make the world go away."*

Regardless of my downheartedness leaving MacArthur's Japan and a facial expression like "The Scream," I was all of a sudden overwhelmed by a towering *Kanagawa* wave-like catharsis and epiphany. I felt a certain degree of purification of emotions, a cleansing and a purging of sordid ideas from my soul.

Woodblock print artist Hokusai created the "Great Wave of *Kanagawa"* during the Edo Period (19th Century).

I finally realized this fact: If my difficult stepfather, who did not accept me, had not been in the springtime of my life, I would never have had the education and adventure of a lifetime, which prepared and propelled me toward all that I've accomplished as an adult. That time, thanks to MacArthur's reconstruction of Japan, allowed me to develop compassion, and come to grips with the absurdity of life and determine the meaning of my existence, realizing that existence precedes essence. If my youth was flawed, it is nothing that I've outgrown. It has served me well.

Therefore, in the spirit of comity and despite the emotional and physical pain I endured, I conclude that one must embrace adversity, pain, failure and burn them as fuel while trekking through life's odyssey.

Eleven-year-old author with brother and friends
in Jinmachi Japan - Summer, 1949

House boy and gardener -
Jinmachi Japan - Winter, 1949

Author - Exiting C-130 aircraft, Ft. Bragg, N.C., August, 1957

Author - 82nd Airborne Jump
School - Ft. Bragg, N.C.,
June, 1957

Author - Undergraduate
Student - Univ. of Maryland -
October, 1960

About the Author

John D. Taylor is a former high school, adult ed and adjunct college history instructor. He has published articles in teachers' periodicals, *Runner's World*, *Reunions Magazine* and an Op-ed piece in *The Washington Post* ("Free For All"). He was the first editor of the *ARK*, a newsletter for the Commonwealth of Virginia's Federation of Humane Societies and author of *Beauregard: Canine Warrior*.

In 1989, John's essay "The Munich Enigma" won a fellowship from the National Endowment for the Humanities.

John received a BA from the University of Maryland, an MEd from the University of Virginia and an MA from Georgetown University. He also served as a court-appointed Humane Investigator and is a veteran of the 82nd Airborne Division.

John Lives in Alexandria, Virginia, with his dog, Tasha.